Let every breath praise the Lord.

Psalm 150

Systema Headquarters also offers:
Vladimir Vasiliev's Award-Winning Instructional Film Collection,
Training at International Seminars,
Training at Russian Martial Art School in Toronto
and with world-wide Affiliates.

For more information or to receive your
Complimentary Newsletter visit:
www.LetEveryBreath.com

LET EVERY BREATH...

SECRETS OF THE RUSSIAN BREATH MASTERS

by Vladimir Vasiliev

with Scott Meredith, Ph.D.

based on the teachings of Mikhail Ryabko

Dear Friends,

I would like to start by expressing my deepest gratitude to my outstanding teacher, colleague and friend – Mikhail Ryabko – an inexhaustible source of knowledge and mastery, as well as wisdom, kindness and love.

I also wish to state my vast appreciation to our writer – Scott Meredith – for his exceptional work. Having become by far one of the most knowledgeable Systema instructors, Scott amazed us with his analytical and literary gift, his insight, his persistence as well as his unprecedented patience and modesty. It is due to Scott's talent and selfless work that what Mikhail and I teach our students is now uncovered on the pages of this book.

I sincerely hope that you find the information useful, that you apply it to your life and that you learn to Let Every Breath... enhance your body and your soul.

Vladimir Vasiliev

About the writer:

Scott Meredith is a certified instructor of SYSTEMA under Vladimir Vasiliev. He is intimately familiar with the languages and cultures of Japan and China and is a lifelong student of martial arts. Scott is a professional technologist who holds a Ph.D. from the Massachusetts Institute of Technology and has worked for 20 years as a senior researcher in human-machine interface technologies for IBM, Apple Computer, and Microsoft.

The exercises, ideas, and suggestions in this book are not intended as a substitute for professional medical advice. Always consult your physician or health care professional before beginning any new exercise technique or exercise program particularly if you are pregnant or nursing, or if you are elderly, or if you have any chronic or recurring medical or psychological conditions. Any application of the exercises, ideas, and suggestions in this book is at the reader's sole discretion and risk.

The author and publisher of this book and their employers and employees make no warranty of any kind in regard to the content of this book including, but not limited to, any implied warranties of merchantability, or fitness for any particular purpose. The author and publisher of this book and their employers and employees are not liable or responsible to any person or entity for any errors contained in this document, or for any special, incidental, or consequential damage caused or alleged to be caused directly or indirectly by the information contained in this book.

Table of Contents

Dedication

This book is dedicated to my great teachers and wonderful friends, Vladimir and Valerie Vasiliev. They have made a contribution of truly historical magnitude to humanity's physical, martial, and spiritual culture and progress by boldly pioneering their astonishing ancient art in the New World.

Acknowledgements

My Systema teachers Vladimir Vasiliev and Mikhail Ryabko are the two great masters and custodians of the Russian Systema methods of health, conditioning, confidence and combat. I owe them a debt beyond measure for giving me the chance to catch a few flames of their beautiful fire.

This book is a joint and group production. Vladimir Vasiliev taught me the methods presented here, and gave unstintingly of his time and effort to explain and refine such understanding as I may have achieved. Valerie Vasiliev was absolutely indispensable, functioning as a helpful translator and uncredited co-author of this book. I often felt abashed that her modestly proffered "suggestions" were invariably more succinctly, accurately and engagingly phrased than anything I was able to produce on my own. She has her own profound literary gift, which may one day shine out openly for all of us to bask in.

Mikhail Ryabko is Godfather and master teacher of the entire worldwide Systema community. In preserving and transmitting the Systema methods, he has set in place a teaching and training revolution that is already starting to rock the world. He also took large increments of his very precious time to consult heavily on every aspect of the core teachings contained here. His spiritual humility and personal gentleness combine with his absolute personal mastery of his arts of health and combat to create an inspirational beacon for the whole Systema community.

This book was greatly enhanced by the tireless and dedicated efforts of Kwan Lee and Kevin Secours, as well as the helpful illustrations by Stelios Dokianakis and Alexei Proger.

While everyone in the Systema community has helped me every step of the way, there are a handful of professional or certified teachers and masters of Systema who have crucially shaped whatever bits of understanding I may have attained of this art. I have been a student of the following extraordinary professional instructors of Systema in some authorized venue, for an extended or significant period along my road. Every one of them is an awesome martial artist and teacher (listed alphabetically): Scott Connor, Terry Cruickshank, Demetry Furman, Sergey Makarenko, Jim King, Konstantin Komarov, Alex Kostic, Kwan Lee, Emmanuel Manolakakis, David Merrell, Daniel Ryabko, Valentin Vasiliev, and James Williams.

Systema is based on a spiritual community of friendship and mutual encouragement. Without the following great friends on the path, my way would have been a lot colder and stonier. The following great people and great friends, and everybody else I ever worked with on the mat or floor in any Systema venue, have all been my advisors, consultants, teachers or just pals at crucial moments. They are the trunk of the Systema tree:

Listed alphabetically – Jesse Barnick, Ed Barton, Janice Bishop, Andrew Cefai, Aran Dharmeratnam, John Elliott, Jacob Goldblatt, Ken J. Good, Anastasia Grouza, Eric Hansen, Alexander Hropak, Mark Jakabcsin, Jérôme Kadian, Khosrow Helly, Brian King, David Kirillov, Victor LoConti, Vali Majd, Scott McQueen, Brad Scornavacco, Bradley Scheel, Jason Scroggins, Arkadiy Stepankovskiy, Kaizen Taki, Martin Wheeler, and Sabrina Williams.

Finally, I want to thank the huge number of wonderful Systema teachers and practitioners who it has been my misfortune never to meet in person, but who have inspired me from afar by their personal example and storied attainments and skill, and also sometimes by their writings on our Systema web forum. There are other great friends, teachers, and training partners, all over the world including Russia, too numerous to list, who've given me some light in the dark. I thank you all!

Chapter One

A Search in Secret Russia

"*A merchant man who went seeking goodly pearls ... found one pearl of great price*" - Matthew 13.44-46

Over the past seven years, I have been on a search in secret Russia. In this book, I offer you the treasure that I found there. The Russia I explored is not only a territory of the earth, not only a place of forests, factories, fields, and churches. It is more than the layered greatness of an ancient civilization partly paved-over by the 20th century. It is also an awe-inspiring world of culture, mind, and spirit.

My exploration brought me a rich harvest – a universal training method for self-improvement that applies to everything in my life. The breath training method of Mikhail Ryabko, Systema Breathing, was secreted away in remote monasteries, guarded over long centuries by the ascetic monks of the ancient Orthodox faith, and honed in epic battles by holy warriors defending Russia's vast and forbidding lands. The teachings survived all that, and then worse – the suppression and distortion by 20th century oppressors, usurpers, and invaders. But this truth's light couldn't be dampened or destroyed entirely. Mikhail Ryabko, the Master Teacher of the ancient Russian Systema Breathing, has now restored this "pearl of great price" to the 21st century, offering us self-understanding and self-mastery. This book will put Mikhail's gift, humbly conveyed from that distant place and those remote times, directly into your hands now.

Before I lay out the method, I want to explain my point of view. I'm a student of Vladimir Vasiliev who is the most senior student of Mikhail Ryabko. Though I'm not a master of this method by any stretch of the imagination, I have seen what it is, and how the masters teach it. Since I know from experience the benefits it brings, I'm excited about sharing it with others. Since I'm not a monk in a monastery or a hermit in a cave, I also know how a typical student can weave Systema Breathing into the fabric of everyday life. I'm going to act as a reporter or travel writer, pointing out what I've seen and explaining secrets from distant times and places. I'm also going to offer personal perspective, memories, and reflections on the path that we'll journey together.

My first steps into the Russian world came via martial arts. I have long been fascinated with martial arts and sports. Though I am not a gifted athlete in any way, as a young teenager I discovered – just through wrestling in gym class and occasional schoolyard spats – that I had a minor talent for fighting. Those trivial experiences piqued my interest in the question of how and why people endlessly come into conflict. Many other challenging episodes, some to be told along the way in this book, combined to stoke my curiosity about the limits of the body's strength and the outer circle of the mind's capacity to endure and overcome the hardships of this "vale of tears" – our human life on earth. So, over the years, I took up the study of many types of martial arts, as a convenient avenue of approach to the questions that nettled me.

In martial arts, I had sometimes seen beautiful and mysterious things. I studied the ancient internal and external arts of China for decades, learning to speak Chinese with native fluency. I did much the same with the traditional Japanese arts and language.

My thirty years' training résumé bristles with the names of famous masters and methods. I saw some greatness in all that. Just as often though, I saw pride, delusion, and empty pageantry. That's the human story - I'm not regretful about anything I've learned or experienced.

However, all along the way, a feeling of unreality nagged. I was always blessed with great teachers. The problem, so I thought, lay in myself. Whether I was sparring in the "external" styles, or meditating and posing in the "internal" styles, I simply could not connect the higher, spiritual aspirations and energies that are espoused in principle by all arts with the harsh realities of human conflict - which I knew lay just outside our charmed training circles. Something always seemed unbalanced. How were we to reconcile loving kindness and decency with effective and completely realistic martial arts? Why did the classical arts feel "cramped and distorted" (Bruce Lee's great words), while the combative arts left me feeling depleted and anxious? So, long before I'd ever heard of the Russian martial arts, feeling more disappointed in my own inadequate powers of comprehension than in the arts themselves, I gradually became simply an observer and tourist, rather than a participant in the martial arts world.

Then when I came, as Dante puts it, "midway upon the journey of life", I found something amazing, that shocked my senses and stunned my mind - the Russian breathing and combative training system of Mikhail Ryabko and Vladimir Vasiliev. I found these teachings to be a pure distillation of a thousand years of the uniquely intense Russian spiritual and physical culture. For the first time, my questions about the link between higher energetics and spirituality, and how those finer things interact with the harsh challenges of physical human existence, were not only being addressed, but finally answered. Answered by actions, answered by results, and answered by open, clear teachings on the floor in front of me - not as legend, hearsay, or comic-book delusions.

Even though I first approached the Russian Systema Breathing through martial arts, and although some of the examples and stories discussed here arise from the practice of combatives, the purpose of the teaching is to enhance your *survival,* whoever you are, whatever you do. Therefore, this book doesn't teach martial arts as commonly understood. Martial arts are mainly applicable to security professionals. Police officers, bodyguards, and military and corrections personnel require these highly specialized skills. *Survival,* on the other hand, is for *everyone.* What I've been taught by the Russian masters has freed my mind, strengthened my body, and cleansed my soul – surely the best foundation for survival and thriving.

In this book, I tell the story (many small stories actually) of my encounter with this hidden Russian world, and all its amazing people and events. I hope to bring the teachings to you with the same clear, humble, and loving ambience in which they were first offered to me. I offer what I saw, what I heard, what I was taught and told – simply my own experience. Considering the newness in the West of the Russian methods of "athletic spirituality" presented here, I imagine there will be something fresh, useful, and interesting for most readers.

Here's a roadmap of our journey. I'll introduce you to my two phenomenal teachers, Mikhail Ryabko and Vladimir Vasiliev. If you don't know those names, you are in for a huge treat. I will describe the simplest, most streamlined breathing method. I'll present the unique Russian melding of physical training and breath control. I'll describe unique methods for learning breath control, timing, coordination, and self-pacing. I will disclose the special methods used in Systema Breathing to understand your own processes of conscious and unconscious tension and relaxation, and to feel and control your internal functions. I'll offer profound insights from interviews with Mikhail Ryabko and Vladimir Vasiliev themselves on the deepest questions that students frequently raise, including the relation of these practices to religion and spirituality.

Before we roll into the full story, let me present you with a snapshot of a mid-morning training session, somewhere near Moscow, with autumn approaching...

The beautiful late-summer forest, a somber edge of tightly pressed silver birch trees, murmured softly outside the high vaulted windows of the Russian training gym. Our small group has traveled from everywhere on earth to meet at this special compound, at the center of a gracious natural park in the Moscow region, Russia. As I stand quietly with my fellow pilgrims on the honorably worn planks of the gym, my eyes and spirit open in wonder as the students of Mikhail Ryabko, the Master Teacher of the Russian Systema, casually and modestly display their awesome skills. Though I've trained in Systema for several years in North America, today at last I can smell and feel the air, and the good earth of Russia, that has nourished their brave and powerful spirit through so many harsh trials.

Let's watch together for a moment. What powers have been passed down through the centuries, from the great cities, the gold-domed cathedrals, the tiny river villages, the hermits' forest huts, and the castle-monasteries of Ancient Russia to shine openly for us that morning, after so many years of darkness?

Endurance: Sergei, short and stocky, accepts full-force punches to his solar plexus from a highly-trained English boxer and heavyweight free-fighting champion. Sergei is enduring force sufficient to kill any ordinary man. He stands calmly and smiles placidly; seeming to sigh almost comfortably as each shocking impact reverberates through the gym. I have the impression that he could break the puncher's wrist with his belly, on the rebound, if he were so inclined. However, his mild and placid expression never hints of the aggression we might expect in so formidable a combat master.

Control: Alexander (Sasha) dives, rolls, and gently falls across the hard bare walls and tough planked floors – something like an acrobat? A Judo master? No, there's something different here. Sasha never makes a sound! He's throwing himself dramatically all over the gym, rebounding off the unforgiving floor and hard-block walls, but all so softly, so quietly. It is pure mastery of motion. Watching Sasha, I have an impression of a perfect sphere, some sort of balloon that never challenges a hard surface, yet cannot be damaged. The clue to his softness is his quietness. He never slaps, clunks, bumps or thumps on any surface. There's only perfect self-control – he has the weightless soft silence of snow falling on snow.

Power: Daniel's light punches and strikes feel like the Kremlin Wall has collapsed on me. They seem somehow gentle on first contact, yet they have a tremendous, surging "after taste" of pure power – I feel every one of my internal organs vibrating at its own distinct frequency! I'm about to pass out – but then, flashing his luminous smile, Daniel, a Russian boy of only sixteen at the time we first met (but the son of a great Russian master), "takes away" my pain and tension with a quick hand motion, scarcely brushing my chest! I straighten up, relieved. More than relieved though, I'm actually beaming, happy and grateful – both for the lesson and the "rescue" from it.

Absolute Mastery: Mikhail Ryabko, Master Teacher of the ancient Russian Systema, allows attacks from anybody. There's nothing pre-planned, yet he seems to know exactly what an attacker will do. He always knows! The attacks come from any direction at any speed, but these experienced fighters might as well send him an advance telegram or flash a warning semaphore – Mikhail always knows exactly what they'll do, where they are aiming, well before their motion begins. Thus, he's never where they think he'll be – with one light step, one simple turn of the waist, head, or wrist the attacker is frozen, always appearing utterly surprised to find himself locked or sent spinning backwards several yards into the arms of the audience.

It is mysterious and almost frightening to watch – but the effect is softened by the aura of kindness, light and peace that always seems to surround this Master warrior.

That is a small, eye-catching sampler of the combative side of Mikhail Ryabko's Systema of combatives and the Systema Breathing on which it is all built, but there's much more to it than that.

There's the light, strong, perfect touch of the students who apply ancient Russian methods of massage to relieve our group of our physical knots, tensions, kinks, and tangles. And there's the truly bizarre yet absolutely real experience of being "put to sleep" – laid gently out on the floor at Mikhail's whim – with each separate muscle lulled beyond the possibility of conscious re-activation by my own will. I feel each muscle has been individually "switched off" by Mikhail's mysterious linkage of his own breath timing to mine, and try as I will, I cannot get up! I can see and hear everything, but I just cannot move. It is a strangely peaceful experience.

Always, there's an incredible alertness – the unobtrusive but unceasing awareness of all Mikhail's students. Their friendly eyes, with casual glances, miss nothing that happens in the gym. A forgotten water bottle, any minor injury, every need, every deed, every physical or mental glitch of pride, pain, or anxiety – seems to flash out to them, signaled in the air somehow, and they respond instantly, quietly, efficiently and modestly to all needs. Among the many Russian Systema teachers, colleagues, students, 'Spetsnaz' (Russian Special Forces) soldiers, friends and family gathered here to work with us, there are no "accidental people" and there are no "accidental moments". Every moment has meaning, every action is purposeful.

There's an equally profound mystery in the realm of medical healing. The same Systema Breath training methods that enable the dramatic physical feats described above are used as the bridge to a deeply spiritual healing power. This is manifested both by Mikhail himself, who has a legion of curative testimonials from patients who have suffered from every imaginable disease, and also by some of his most senior students.

Dr. Yuri Vedov is a physician practicing medicine at St. John's clinic in Moscow. He is unusual in that he has received full professional training in clinical medicine, holding an MD degree, and is also a seminary graduate, schooled in the ancient Russian Orthodox Christianity. He is also a student of Mikhail Ryabko and has gone perhaps farther than anybody except Mikhail himself in integrating the specific breath, body, and energetic practices of ancient Russia with modern clinical diagnostic and healing perspectives. He is a bold medical pioneer in that he assesses the severely ill patients who seek him out in both physiological and spiritual terms. He prescribes breathing regimens together with prayer to clean disease from both the body and soul.

Dr. Vedov's results are dramatic and compelling. He has successfully treated endometriosis, uterine dystrophy, ovarian swelling and cysts, as well as many forms of cancer. After initial assessment, which includes review of all pre-existing clinical records and previous diagnoses, as well as a thorough physical examination and probing of a new patient's state of mind and spirit, Dr. Vedov will usually prescribe a specific, customized breathing practice regimen, derived from Mikhail's teachings.

Daily breathwork, says Dr. Vedov, over several weeks (or months, for cases of extreme malignant cancers) cleanses both the patient's consciousness (the source of disease) and body (the observable site where disturbance, uncleanliness, or imbalance of the psyche is ultimately displayed). By this means, he has cured "terminal" cancer patients for whom all chemotherapy, radiation, and surgical treatments had been discontinued as utterly hopeless!

Mikhail Ryabko is also able to effect such cures with his personal intervention and direct transfer of spiritual energy to an individual patient. Sadly though, there's only one Mikhail – "not enough to go around" in this world full of sickness and suffering. Therefore, Dr. Vedov is teaching patients to perform self-healing, by relying, with God's help, on their own personal diligence.

Dr. Vedov spent over twenty years undergoing advanced yogic and energetic training in India. He is fluent in the languages of India and has been directly learning from the mysterious and powerful teachers of India. However, he has expressed his profound conviction that none of the startling practices and apparent medical and spiritual miracles he witnessed in his long years of work there compare with the profundity of the Russian Systema rooted in Orthodox Christianity. It's a case of finding diamonds buried in your own backyard. With his vast experience, profound intellect, and humble faith, Dr. Vedov has gone farther than anyone else both in understanding the subtle nuances and profound depths of Mikhail's ancient teachings and in applying them to the troubles of modern life. We hope that he will continue his unique synthesis of medical practice supported by spiritual devotion. It is likely that one day he will summarize it all for us in a book that goes far beyond the scope of this present introductory effort!

I have seen and experienced everything described above, and much more, in my travels to Russia. Everyone who touches the dark rich Russian soil feels the life and spirit that this culture emanates. When we are with Mikhail Ryabko, it all seems distilled to a pure, concentrated essence. Probably due to Mikhail's profound commitment to prayer and the religious life, he generates a tangible "spiritual presence" that far transcends the direct application of his power for combat or self-defense. What I have seen and partially described above is pure spirit, projected via the human body. And we must finally live by the spirit only – for all else perishes.

Now your question is – how exactly is that mastery achieved? What's the foundation? Mikhail hides nothing and will happily reveal to anyone with sincere interest, even a visitor, the same teaching received by his closest veteran students and colleagues.

And here is the teaching:

The foundation is breathing. The mastery begins there.

You've now read the accounts of the great Russian combat masters and healers, and their students, and you may be wondering how the mastery they display relates to your own life. Those of us who aren't martial artists are still warriors facing our own life challenges in our own way. Those among us who aren't doctors or professional healers need to protect the health of our families and of ourselves. We need a simple source of power to replenish our bodies, minds and spirits. Mikhail Ryabko teaches how to access that power, and he and his students easily and openly demonstrate the physical and spiritual benefits of embracing breath as the vehicle of self-mastery. And – beyond the gateway of the breath lies a vast open country of pure spirit.

So let's explore our breathing now, and ride it as far as we can.

Chapter Two

The Teachers Appear

"*Yet shall not thy teachers be removed into a corner any more, but thine eyes shall see thy teachers*" - Isaiah 30.20

Mikhail Ryabko is the living link between the mysterious past of the ancient Russian breathing system and the modern training regimens (combative, healing, and spiritual) based on them. Mikhail is a larger-than-life presence in every sense. But before I met Mikhail, I was introduced to Systema by another amazing figure – Vladimir Vasiliev.

Vladimir Vasiliev

The biographical record on Vladimir Vasiliev shows less detail than we curious students would like. Due to his long history of classified work in specialized anti-terror intelligence circles of the secretive former Soviet Union, little more of his personal history than the following basic sketch can be told.

He was born in Tver, a city of ancient vintage lying on the main roads between Moscow and St. Petersburg, through which flow three great rivers of Russia: the Volga, the Tvercza and the Tmakee. The city is surrounded by forest, and is a famous hunting region even today.

As a young man, Vladimir joined the Army, and his obvious talent soon resulted in his induction to one of the few Special

Operations Units, forming an elite of the elite, used in the highest-risk missions. The soldiers of these units went through extreme training in the full spectrum of physical and psychological capacities. After mastering the traditional Russian fighting styles, they continuously honed their skills in covert military operations and personal protection of top government and military personnel.

Vladimir's work spans ten years of extensive military service with the Special Operations Unit, including regular high-risk covert assignments. In the early 1990's, Vladimir moved to Canada, and in 1993 founded the first school of Russian Martial Art outside Russia. By the year 2006, he has personally trained and certified over 100 qualified Russian Martial Art instructors in over a dozen countries, and has created an award-winning instructional film collection.

I've met many martial arts masters and other great, pre-eminent figures in every field. Yet, meeting Vladimir for the first time is different. In describing him, my mind falters a bit; my fingers stumble on the keyboard – something radically powerful and different shines out from this cheerful and friendly Russian gentleman. My body and spirit intuited his radiance even before my mind grasped that I had found a truly great master.

A great master – that's my view. Nobody I know who's worked with Vladimir would dispute the label for an instant. Yet, Vladimir himself wouldn't accept it. He frequently tells his students of his own great senior teachers, such as Mikhail Ryabko, and past colleagues. I never know how to respond to his modesty, though I understand his feeling – being worshiped and admired leads to pride – and thus to obstruction of the spirit and then the body. Both Russian culture and Systema training spirit emphasize humility and community. That's why no ranks or belts divide the students into seniority levels. Anyway, Vladimir is an extraordinary master, teacher, and human being. Bear with me while I describe the first time I met him. There's a lesson in it.

I live near Seattle, across the North American continent from Vladimir's Toronto Russian Martial Art school. I made my first visit to Vladimir's Russian Martial Art (RMA) school in mid-2000. I had seen a brief mention of Systema in a martial arts magazine almost a year prior, but hadn't organized myself to visit until the following summer. After reading about him, I initially contented myself with ordering a few of Vladimir's videos. When I saw them, an inner voice told me – something's different here.

In my more than thirty years' pursuit of martial arts instruction and spiritual insight, I'd always sought an ultimately great teacher, one who could speak to the soul and teach transcendence of the body's physical limits. I felt that martial arts ability could serve as a tangible grounding for spiritual truth. Not that just anybody who can fight well is necessarily a great spiritual figure, but profound soul-teaching can be given in forms other than words. I felt that martial arts could be a vehicle for spiritual demonstration.

Through the years, I found some fantastic near-misses. I put myself in the hands of many hugely skilled and large-hearted people, who lent their blood, sweat and tears to the task of unlocking my body and magnifying my soul. But, I had to keep moving on, always seeking, never finding.

Beyond pure combative mastery, I had no particular idea in mind for exactly who such a model teacher would be - no further specifications for the appearance or behavior of the one I sought. I was just sure I'd know him when I saw him… or perhaps I should say, when he saw me.

Still, I was hesitant to visit Vladimir's school for on-site training. After a few years of wild, no-rules sparring training (flowing blood, flying teeth, etc.) as a teen, under a roguishly tough Kung-Fu teacher, most of my training had shied definitively to the softer, contemplative side of the arts. What would the tough

Systema fighters in Toronto do to a newbie? Obviously they'd eat me alive. With that psychological underpinning, I easily found any excuse to keep myself safely several thousand miles away.

But as the months dragged, the thoughts nagged – and Vladimir's Systema videos tugged at me. Who really is this guy? Why does his work look ... different? Finally in the spring of 2000, I bought a ticket to Toronto for a summer visit. I felt foolish – what was I seeking? Why should I want to learn to fight anyway, even if I could? And if I didn't care about combatives, why should I darken Vlad's doorframe at all?

I had called the school a couple of months prior and been assured that Vladimir would be teaching his normal routine – every class – through late July and August. I didn't commit to any a particular date. I didn't get back in touch with the school, and I didn't notify anybody in Toronto about my visit.

I got in on a Sunday evening, and spent a nervous night in a nearby cheerfully downscale motel. Come the dawn, it was time to roll for my first class. By then, I was thinking – why bother these guys with my ethereal questing? As I locked the motel door and scooted downstairs to the parking lot, I thought up an easy "out" – I would say I'd come only to watch a single class. I'd observe a class, and, flinging a quick 'Do svidanya!' over my shoulder, I'd be out of there and back home the same evening.

I had a feeling of futility. What's the point? What can this teacher possibly have different from all the other great ones I've seen and felt? It's all the same. Each one is great in his unique way, yet ... they're all the same. None of them had ever truly reached my mind and soul.

I always arrive very early for anything. I found the RMA school's section of the little warehouse row easily enough and wheeled into one of the diagonal parking slots more than forty minutes before the start of class. There was a scattering of other cars parked adjacent to mine, evidently belonging to other people doing other things, as the RMA school was dark and locked tight. There was nothing conspicuous about my car nor was it isolated as the only car in that parking section. A weedy railroad track stretched to infinity on the other side of the fence.

I'd spoken to someone at the school only once, more than three months prior, and I had never spoken to Vladimir personally. I hadn't told them my precise arrival date, and nobody was expecting me.

It was a gorgeous morning - blue sky, warm breeze, birds chirping - when they could be heard over the roar of occasional freight trains hammering past thirty feet away. Too nice a day to wait in the car.

The edge of the parking area, opposite to the RMA school and the neighboring ballet academy, was bounded by a low wall. Behind the wall, overhanging the front of my nosed-in car, was a large, weepy overgrown tree. I sat in the shady nook at the tree's foot. The row of parked cars, mostly blocked my view of the drive-way separating the parking slots from the row of units housing the dance and RMA school. The tree's leafy, shaggy branches overhung me completely as I sat cross-legged, low and quiet. I wasn't trying to hide myself. I just wanted to be comfortable.

So a silly thought popped up - what makes a master anyway? Is it mental or physical? Is it fighting or avoidance of fighting? Or could it be just pure awareness? Doesn't real mastery extend beyond the practice mat? I even thought "If this man is a true master, then although I'm invisible from the driveway, and though many other cars have now cruised past me obliviously and nobody has seen me... if he's a true master, he'll see me. He'll know there's somebody here."

I chided myself - who are you to judge a famous teacher in this arbitrary way? What difference would it make, even if he does drive right on past? It's obvious from the videos that he can fight, and that's enough. Yet I couldn't stop wondering about it, as I heard the approach of another vehicle. I watched my narrowly visible road-slice.

As the nose of a Land-Rover passed my view, I saw the driver. It was Vladimir – I recognized him from the training videos. Just as he drove past, he simply turned his head and looked directly at me.

He "saw" me.

He showed no particular reaction. It was not a hostile or "check you out" type of glance. It was pure awareness in action. I had never experienced that in its full purity before – not in all my prior training. My first meeting with the teacher had no more substance than that single moment, but it rocked my world.

Vladimir was not swiveling his head around manically searching for snipers. He was not going through the rote of a hyper-aware Special Operative. He was just driving. He was simply, as Mikhail Ryabko likes to say about normal people performing simple actions, "buttering his toast".

But while acting "normal", he somehow knew I was there. His mild and friendly look said only "Yes. I see you. I know you are sitting there". But it was shocking on an energetic level; I felt a whole-body resonance. It was as though an invisible string had gently turned his head at precisely the right instant. His quiet and natural look caught me and held me completely.

Even now, after six years of close association with Vladimir, I haven't come close to unraveling the mystery of this great teacher. But I knew I had found a genuinely great master. I was psychologically floored. Here for the first time in my life, was a perfect, and perfectly natural, demonstration of absolute awareness. Vladimir had demonstrated the complete Systema teaching to me in the first two seconds of my first visit, in the parking lot, before I ever entered the school.

I decided to participate after all, of course, and I went through that entire first class floating in a trance. I won't detail the specifics of what Vladimir teaches in martial arts. It is enough to say that Systema offers a unique combination of relaxation with devastating practical combative effect. Vladimir emphasizes the defensive aspects in his teaching, and often reminds us that Systema is a survival system – intended to strengthen the individual's body, mind, and spirit. Strong individuals are the foundation for building stronger families, communities, and nations.

Getting dumped on the floor and most amusingly folded, spindled, and twisted by the various seniors and juniors in more ways than I would have thought possible, I found myself swirling in a weird psychological and physical blur of very friendly people administering very tough lessons.

Throughout that morning's class, every fifteen minutes or so, Vladimir would stop the general practice action to perform a jaw-dropping "live" demonstration, with advanced students. Regardless of the normal dynamics of teacher-student interaction, what he did with his awareness, his positioning, his timing, his power, and his kinetic creativity appeared to lie right on the raw edge of physical impossibility. He radiated an astonishing and obvious special mastery.

The martial arts work of Systema is built on four basic principles – breathing, relaxation, natural body position, and movement. You can't relax without breathing, you can't achieve natural posture without relaxation, and only once you have the right form in a stationary position can you hope to move it through space. This book is devoted to breathing – the first of the basic principles, the one that enters us first and underlies all of Systema and life itself. The breathwork foundation of the Systema combative system is called Systema Breathing, and it applies to all of life, far beyond the narrow scope of combatives. I'm not going to explore the Russian Systema martial arts any further in this book beyond this chapter, but clearly breath is the foundational element of Vladimir's jaw-dropping combative artistry.

How good is Vladimir? Let me attempt an analogy. The 1950's epic movie "The Ten Commandments" depicts the total destruction of the Egyptian Pharoah's army. Thousands of horses, men, chariots, and miscellaneous military hardware are shown smashed, with the fragments swirling in the waves of the Red Sea. Having parted spectacularly for Moses a moment earlier, the walls of water have now slammed together after the Pharoah Ramses, from his clifftop command perch, ordered his entire horde into the pursuit. This military disaster came hard on the heels of the various plagues and other torments that Moses had foretold earlier. Ramses watches the entire army of Egypt destroyed instantaneously in the sea, and then drags himself back, the lone surviving chariot, to his now-empty palace.

As he slumps on the gleaming marble throne, he's surrounded by ebony and black-granite statues of Isis and Anubis, and all the other symbols to which he's prayed for victory and power. His wife the queen enters the throne room and begins to carp: "Well? Didn't you kill Moses? And you call yourself a man? The Mighty Pharaoh, eh? Bah!" But at this point Pharoah is far beyond those egotistical concerns. He slowly raises his head and, fixing her with a thousand-mile stare, he mutters: "His God ... IS God!"

Strange as it sounds, the first time I saw Vladimir doing his combative work in person, the same light-has-finally-dawned mentality branded me permanently. Exactly this line spontaneously came to me: "His martial art... IS martial art!"

Despite the curtain that must be drawn over some details of his history, Vladimir often draws from his seemingly infinite store of incredibly amusing and spectacular anecdotes about his past. Some day a great writer will draw more of those out of him for the historical record. Since this book is teaching you how to breathe, I'll resist the temptation to dive into that project! For now, you only need to realize that Vladimir himself attributes whatever mastery of martial arts, and of life, that others (like me) may ascribe to him largely to an understanding of breath as the bridge between body and psyche.

Mikhail Ryabko

Now that I've introduced Vladimir you may want to lean back, take a deep breath, and exclaim to yourself "Nothing could top that!"

But there's more! Mikhail Ryabko was one of Vladimir's own teachers during his formative years in Russia. He was possibly the greatest single influence on the mastery that Vladimir came to embody. Mikhail functions at a level of personal mastery that we associate with ancient legends and stories of classical warrior saints. His appearance is extremely unassuming, but his combative and healing work, as well as his spiritual presence, resonates with pure power.

Even less seems to be publicly known of Mikhail's personal history than of Vladimir's. We know only that he was trained from the age of five by one of Stalin's personal bodyguards, and was inducted to Spetsnaz at the age of fifteen. He has been a tactical commander of hostage-rescue teams, counter-terrorist operations, and armed criminal neutralization. Mikhail resides in Moscow, holds the rank of Colonel and serves as a Special Advisor to the Minister of Justice of the Russian Federation. He continues to train his many students as the Master Teacher of Systema. He has authored a textbook on Tactics of Special Operations. He has been in numerous military campaigns and holds many government medals and awards.

Beyond the brief biographical facts, Mikhail is a living legend. There are hundreds of stories and testimonials from people in all walks of Russian life as to Mikhail's healing powers, combative mastery, and spiritual radiance. But with all the adulation and publicity naturally accumulating around him, he remains an incredibly modest and touchingly shy figure. His sweet, childlike face always appears in any group dignitary picture as the least likely appearance for a master martial artist or decorated military specialist. He looks like a village priest or a simple country doctor.

Mikhail is clearly functioning at a non-ordinary level of highly spiritual intuition. That can be seen both in his combative work where he never exerts himself in the slightest degree – because he always knows where an assailant will be, and what he will attempt, long before any physical motion has begun. It is also obvious from his healing work, where he shows an empathic quality of deep listening and seeming to know a person's body much better than they do themselves.

In my mid-teens, I got into a horrific auto-crash. In those Dark Ages when seat belts were never worn and could (sometimes) be located only by plunging your arm to the shoulder between the front seat cushions, it never occurred to me that I'd end up propelled head first through the windshield, scattering it in shards all over the road, and catapulting straight over the hood and hard down onto the pavement – by collision with a speeding drunk driver. I was unconscious, with my jaw and face more or less destroyed. Blood and teeth and other nasty stuff littered the pavement. There was a fade to black, and then I found myself staring into the surgical spotlight on the emergency room ceiling, my face rocking in the firm but gentle hands of an oral surgeon, who managed to piece back together the remnants of my jaw, and to reinsert the dislodged teeth. The attending ER doctor stood by to observe the oral surgeon's work, and spoke prophetically: "He's the best oral surgeon in this state, but in your forties, you're going to start losing those teeth".

Now fast-forward thirty years, and flip the scene to Toronto, the RMA school where Mikhail has graced us in most recent years with his teaching. I'd been at Vladimir's school for a week of training, to culminate with Mikhail's special seminar. After a rough but thrilling training day, I returned to my hotel tired and happy. As fate would have it, brushing my teeth that evening – whoops! Suddenly there it went, my lower front-center tooth, one of those rearranged by the accident, right down the drain. There was no connection to the day's training activities whatsoever – it was just that tooth's time to move on – payback for putting it through the windshield those many decades before. It was no big deal, as it was in the lower jaw, not very noticeable, and not painful.

The next morning, I arrived early, admitted to the gym by the assistant instructor, along with some classmates. I changed, and got out on the floor with the early crowd to warm up, chat, and try some moves with various people, as usual. Vladimir and Mikhail had not yet arrived. On a seminar day, the room crowds-up fast. I was in a far corner, working with somebody, my back turned to the entrance, facing the mirrors, surrounded by rolling, stretching, large bodies. Remember that my missing tooth, although in the front-center, was from my lower jaw, so it wasn't noticeable unless I smiled. Luckily, I'm a serious guy, so nobody took any notice whatsoever.

Suddenly, there was a tap on my shoulder – Mikhail had come up right behind me! Oh! Yes? What? I hadn't even seen him come into the school. Mikhail pointed directly to my lower jaw. There was no interpreter present – it seemed Mikhail had come straight from the front door directly to my place on the mat! He pointed to my face and showed his own teeth, clearly meaning to ask "What happened?"

Think of it – I was at the back of the room, and I was one of eighty students he'd been working with that weekend! This incident absolutely stupefied me, but it was simply another proof of Mikhail's legendary powers of observation and sensitivity.

Mikhail is a devout follower of the Russian Orthodox Church, while opening his teaching to followers of all religions and of no religion, throughout the world. Mikhail has always emphasized religion and spirituality as the "strategic" foundation of his abilities, and the breathwork presented in this book forms his primary set of training "tactics".

The anecdotes about Mikhail are legion! I could easily fill this book or another with them. However, Mikhail always discourages personal attention and elaborate biographies, saying they derive from a "Hollywood" mentality. He frequently says: "Nothing is personal – everything is from God." So, you'll have to contain your curiosity for now.

Let's move on to the breath training!

Chapter Three

The Seven Principles

"*Wisdom hath builded her house, she hath hewn out her seven pillars*"
- Proverbs, 9.1

The Russian Breathing System or Systema Breathing applies to every waking moment of your life! You might wonder how any system can cover so much. After all, life is infinitely variable. The Principles in this chapter provide the foundation for both our breathing practice and all our work in daily life. Remember that your breath is your life. So, these Principles are "Laws of Life" that stand behind and beyond any particular exercise. They apply to everything introduced in this book. I'll refer back to the Principles many times as specific work and practices are introduced in following chapters.

Before I get to the Principles, I'd like to cover some important introductory ideas. The big problem we have with using our powers fully in daily life is that we often hold and obstruct our breath without even noticing.

So why don't we breathe properly? There are
two basic types of obstructions:

(1) Psychological breath disruption
You usually disrupt your breathing cycle in response to any

stressful factor when something unexpected happens (with your tense mental or physical reaction) or due to psychological habits, such as anxiety and fear. These disruptions may be unconscious reactions to a sudden movement or sound, or an intense emotion. Even simple actions can trigger breath disruptions. For example, signing a check or putting a key into a lock or a sudden noise behind you may lead to tension and breath blockage, even if no real threat exists.

(2) Physical breath disruption

You may have areas of restriction in your body. You may have areas of physical tension, disease, pain or fatigue that block the natural flow of your breath. Areas of physical blockage due to tension, bad posture or injury can persist over years. The breathing practices introduced in this book will assist you to overcome all these impediments.

Listen-UP!

Systema Breathing therefore emphasizes two basic requirements:

- Your breathing continues constantly, no matter what
- Your breath permeates your entire body

Helping you achieve these fundamental conditions is the primary focus of this book. It is very simple. But when you watch yourself doing everyday activities or going through the drills taught in this book, you'll quickly realize how hard it can be to achieve these two goals. And you'll understand that tremendous power can be derived from their mastery.

Systema Breathing Compared to Yoga and Qi Gong

Historically, many different methods for training breath, motion, and posture have been taught. These methods often come with impressive historical credentials, and are often connected to the medical and religious traditions of India and China. In the Chinese language, *qi gong* refers to a large family of practices for enhancing energy and health through breathing and special motions. The *pranayama* and *kundalini* practices of Indian yoga likewise incorporate specialized breath patterns together with special postures and motions that are thought to promote health and spiritual growth. Because all deal with breath, these practices may **superficially** seem similar to the Russian work. In fact however, the philosophy, focus, and practice of Systema Breathing differ fundamentally from any other method.

The methods of yoga and *qi gong* gradually cultivate an awareness of breath by means of an extended series of complicated postures. These methods often require extraordinary attention to inner states and extreme physiological control. In the Russian System, however, the breath alone is primary.

Listen-UP!

Everything great is simple. We don't need to do anything extreme that deviates hugely from daily life. We already have what we need.

Systema only teaches us to extend our awareness and practical usage of what we already have. Systema Breathing does not teach intricate or complex physical postures. Finally, Mikhail does not refer to imaginary deep channels of supernatural energy in the body, nor does his method involve any occult concepts.

The postures, exercises, and processes of the Ryabko System are simple in structure and appearance. The benefits come as you begin to better understand your natural body, mind and emotions under difficult but controlled conditions. The Russian masters accept that reality can be harsh. Some people may believe they can achieve a mystical state of perfect physical balance and mental elevation in their quiet rooms, with soft carpets, gentle background music and wafting incense. But do they know how they'll hold up when cold, hungry, or under extreme stress? How well do mystical experiences apply to work frustrations, the exhaustion of raising children, or self-defense emergencies?

Nobody wants to suffer, but a degree of controlled stress in training can teach us a lot. Systema Breathing safely simulates the extreme stresses of life, allowing us to meet and overcome them under the manageable conditions of our training environment, and in so doing, prepares us for the inevitable stressful encounters of our everyday lives.

Systema offers you challenges that lie right at the edge of your current strength level. This is done with commonplace, entirely safe postures and sequences. These postures are so simple that anybody can execute them, with no special training, and in any ordinary environment.

Breath Circulation

Breathing is more than just a mechanical process, more than merely filling your lungs as two bags of air. A machine like bellows for fire or an iron lung might work in that *mechanical* way. In living people, however, breathing is a complicated chemical process that involves every cell in our bodies, with every breath we take.

As we train in Systema Breathing, we begin to feel the truth that breath is the major *physiological* process of the body. Breathing connects the Respiratory System to the body's other six major physiological systems (Circulatory, Muscular-skeletal, Nervous, Endocrine, Digestive, and Genital-urinary). Your breath literally does not stop at your lungs! When you understand that "simple" idea and begin to feel it, you've taken your first big step in your training journey. The inhalation continues into all tissues, and exhalation expels wastes from all the other systems.

The Seven Principles:

1. Nose and Mouth

The Principle of Nose Inhalation and Mouth Exhalation: For all the exercises described in this book, you should always inhale through the nose, and exhale through the mouth.

When you inhale through your nose, you will notice that your body has more control of the volume and speed of air intake. As a result, the muscles affecting the lungs tend to relax more, without the flinching and sporadic seizing that often accompanies inhaling through the mouth. This allows you to take fuller breaths.

Try-It-Now!

Perform a few cycles of long, deep breathing. At first use only your mouth, and then switch to using only your nose. You will likely begin to feel anxiety building in the chest when inhaling through your mouth, especially around the heart. In contrast, you may notice a sense of relaxation spreading through your body when you inhale through the nose.

Inhaling through the nose is the first step in optimizing control of your own body. In a stressful situation, this breathing method alone can be used to calm your mind and prepare yourself to perform an important task. The nose also performs important filtration and temperature regulation of incoming air.

Try the same type of comparison with your exhalation. You will begin to notice that exhaling through your mouth allows a more comfortable and relaxing expulsion of air. Exhaling through your nose tends to increase anxiety and create a feeling that you can't exhale quickly or fully enough.

Even casual experimentation with inhaling through the nose and exhaling through the mouth will probably convince you of the naturalness of this method. This principle applies at all times during training of Systema Breathing, and also during any stressful life situation. Of course, we all know there are social situations in daily life when exhaling through the mouth may not be entirely appropriate. At those times, remember some other useful ideas taught by Vladimir and Mikhail: Be flexible. Don't be fanatical. Act normal!

2. Leading

The Principle of Breath Leading: Most of the breathing exercises taught in this book are performed in combination with some physical activity. Respiration and physical activity are a unified process. However, when performing a physical action, the breathing is the more important component.

Systema Breathing teaches us to begin any exercise motion or cycle with a breath action (inhalation or exhalation) – before the physical motion starts. **Only when your breath action has begun should the physical movement "tag along".** There should be a very brief lag time between the breath action and the physical motion. Use your breath to pull or push all physical motions.

Think of how the engine of a train works. Most locomotive engines pull with a "sliding coupler". This is a special linking device between train cars that allows the engine to begin its own movement, and then to gradually begin to pull the next wagon, which follows along naturally. Eventually, every wagon in the train begins to move, each with a slight lag-time relative to its predecessor. Finally, thousands of tons of steel (the entire train) stream smoothly along. In the same way, breathing is the engine that has to exert a leading pull on your body's physical work.

The Principle of Breath Leading reminds us that breathing has the priority in all physical work and in all exercises of the

Systema Breathing. We are not trying to build up our muscles for show. Full and free breathing, as emphasized in the other Principles, is choked off by unconscious or unwanted tension or stress in the body. To breathe right, we must relax. Start any activity with relaxed breathing.

3. Sufficiency

The Principle of Intake Sufficiency: A person attempting to breathe fully and deeply usually inhales as much air as possible. That's natural, but it's a mistake! Forceful over-inhalation causes instant tension in the neck and collarbone area. That pressure, in turn, cramps the breathing. Your body can become completely locked-up and obstructed by this practice. Over time, you end up with inadequate oxygen, inefficiently utilized.

Therefore, you should not try to inhale as much air as you can hold. Instead, you should only inhale as much air as necessary for the work you are engaged in, just as much air as your body needs at a particular time. Try to be sensitive to what your body is really asking for. Take just the necessary amount of air, and smoothly pass it through all parts of your body. That will keep you relaxed and gradually make your breathing full and appropriate to your task or situation. But you cannot do this if you cut your inhalation and exhalation short either.

In the natural breathing of Systema, we remain relaxed. So, without pressure in your neck and collarbones, and without any forcing, you should allow your body to inhale just as much as it wants. As you inhale, relax your body. At the same time, try to feel that the inhaled air is softly and smoothly flowing throughout your entire body. The breath will naturally flow to the softer, more relaxed parts of the body. It will avoid all tension and harder areas. After a natural pause, when you exhale, the air should softly and smoothly exit from all parts of your body, without any extreme force or stress.

Try-It-Now!

1. Take a very full breath – feel how this tends to over-inflate the top part of the lungs, and how this tenses your neck, shoulder, and chest muscles. Exhale.
2. Now take in just as much air as you need right now – notice it will not feel as full, but the inhalation is deep and quiet. Exhale again.
3. Now allow the next breath to follow, in the same quiet and relaxed manner. If you did the 2nd "just enough" inhale properly, you will naturally inhale just a bit more air because your upper body muscles will be relaxed, thus effortlessly permitting a naturally enhanced intake capacity.

If you breathe this way, your body starts to relax. This causes your body to rid itself of chronic tensions. You will also find yourself becoming more aware of tension that you might never have consciously noticed. Your breathing actions will naturally deepen and lengthen. That leads to a natural increase in the amount of inhaled air. When that natural increase begins for you, allow it fully. This gradual expansion of your breath capacity is very different from forceful over-inhalation. As your capacity begins to expand naturally, don't suppress or obstruct your breathing either!

4. Continuity

The Principle of Breath Continuity: Your breath must never be stopped, interrupted, or suppressed. Inhale and exhale continuously. Don't hold your breath or stop it, unless you have a special training purpose (as discussed in the following chapter).

To understand the point, consider some real-life situations when stopping and suppression of breathing often occur. It might be a scare connected with an unexpected sound ("BOO!"), or an abrupt movement, or you stumbling. Also, notice your breathing when you have to concentrate on something, like inserting a thread into a needle, or keying in a phone number, or pouring from a teapot – are you blocking your own breathing then?

Pay attention to any cramped, painful, or tired part of your body. Figure out whether you are really breathing freely through each part. Sometimes you can feel tension that is blocking your breath flow. Once you begin practicing the Systema Breathing exercises, you will notice more and more of your breath stoppages and you will learn how to immediately restore continuity. Learning to push your breathing through any area where it is blocked or interrupted is a key skill in Systema Breathing. With practice, you should be able to feel the continuous flow of oxygen and the energy it carries!

5. Pendulum

The Principle of the Pendulum: A pendulum moves in a simple continuous cycle, extending and retreating, back and forth. Breathing is analogous to this kind of cyclic motion. Think of the extreme end of one swing of the pendulum. It seems to pause for a microsecond as it reaches fullest extension. In breathing, we should pay attention to the very end of each inhale or exhale action. Just before an inhale or exhale action reaches its natural completion, just prior to the natural pause before the start of the next action, is an important time. The very end of an inhale action is when the greatest flow of oxygen and energy permeates the body tissues.

The *Pendulum Principle* of the Systema Breathing teaches that breathing should be smooth and steady. Do not begin to exhale before you complete your inhalation, and vice versa.

This exercise helps us "get the feel" for the change-over point. We learn from experience that prolonging the final steps of inhalation and exhalation can be done naturally, without any forcing. If the final steps of inhalation and exhalation are missing, or cut short, or sped up, your breathing won't be smooth.

Imagine a pendulum that hits a barrier before reaching the natural end of its swing. After such an impact, it will be forced to change its direction abruptly. That is an example of forced change. But if the pendulum is moving freely, with no obstruction, then after reaching the end of its momentum in one direction, it smoothly changes its motion back towards the other side. The position of the pendulum at its extreme is like the natural breath pause (not forced stoppage) that lies between inhalation and exhalation.

Try-It-Now!

1. From any relaxed pose (sitting or standing normally), stay relaxed and inhale a comfortable amount of air.
2. When you feel that the inhalation reaches its natural completion, very gently prolong the inhalation just a bit, in a comfortable way, without noticeable pressure.
3. When you feel that prolongation would introduce tension, allow the cycle to reverse itself naturally by beginning the exhalation.
4. At the bottom of the exhale, sense the natural pause before continuing at a normal rhythm.

6. Independence

The Principle of Breath Independence: Your physical actions should not be invariably linked to any single phase of your breathing (inhalation, exhalation, or pausing). You should not form a training habit of always connecting inhalation or exhalation to any particular activity.

For example, imagine that you are in a fight and need to punch. It could happen at a moment of your natural inhalation. But if your prior training has created a strong habit of punching only on exhalation, you may be delayed or confused in your response, or you'll simply fail to execute a strong punch. Habitual dependencies like that can lead to interruption of breathing; stoppage of breath; hesitation in movement; loss of energy; loss of balance; and other harmful results.

To avoid these harmful habits and make your breathing truly independent of your actions, you should perform breathing exercises with frequent changes of breathing phase. For example, if you are doing pushups (introduced in Chapter 5) by lowering your body on inhalation, and raising your body on exhalation, you should perform the same number of pushups with the breathing phases reversed (lowering your body upon exhalation and raising it upon inhalation). Watch for the many good exercises to develop *Breath Independence* that are presented in later chapters.

7. No Tension

The Principle of Non-Tension: As explained above, all exercises described in this chapter are for controlling breath, relaxing the body, strengthening the tendons and ligaments and very importantly, strengthening your psyche. Your muscles should be only minimally involved. That means your body needs to be relaxed at all times, even while performing the hardest work (such as raising yourself in a pushup). Especially in the beginning, you will need to check your own relaxation. If your muscles are over-involved, or if you are unconsciously tensing the muscles uninvolved in this particular exercise, you will tire very quickly. Relaxation lets us practice long enough to begin the serious breath work. The Principle of Non-Tension will be explained and exemplified extensively in the following chapters.

Some Extras

The Seven Principles above are the heart and soul of Systema Breathing. In addition to those, there are some other training ideas and general good advice that will apply to most of the practice methods. These will be introduced throughout the book, wherever they apply. For now, here are a couple of extra training ideas that supplement the Seven Principles.

Audible Breathing

A good way to understand the *Principle of Breath Continuity* is to feel your respiration with "audible breathing". In Audible Breathing, you make soft sounds as you inhale and exhale. This helps you pay closer attention to your breathing. Audible breathing also makes it easier to break through breath blockage in suppressed, painful, and stressed areas.

Audible Breathing is not a matter of making loud, violent noises. It does not involve shouting from the throat. Very loud breathing can become overly forceful, which causes dizziness, tension and other unpleasant feelings. Audible breathing should sound (and feel) like a person who is gently trying to ease some pain, or relieve fatigue, in any part of the body. It is similar to the sounds you make instinctively when you are lifting something heavy, or when sitting down after hard work – these are natural relaxation responses of your breath, voice and body.

As you begin your practice of audible breathing, it will be noticeable to anybody standing near you (when you practice). But, over time, as you gain greater mastery, your breath will get calmer and calmer. Gradually, the sound will naturally become softer and softer, until bystanders can't hear your breath any longer. Then you will have really achieved something!

A Special Principle

Now I'll introduce one final special "Principle"– Enjoy! By that Mikhail means, don't be fanatical. Smile as you probe your own limitations. And be happy as you notice your expanding powers. Joy comes from doing the right things in life. To do right things for others, you need to be a healthy, strong and humble individual. Becoming your best self requires mastery of breath. Just remember to have some fun along the way.

Chapter Four

The Fundamental Practice of Relaxed Breathing

"And the Lord formed man of the dust of the ground, and breathed into his nostrils the breath of life" - Genesis 2.7

Now let's get to work with a simple method which embodies all the seven Principles of Systema Breathing. Until you become very advanced (and probably even after that), you should always begin any practice session with the Fundamental Practice of Relaxed Breathing. You may also wish to begin your day with the Fundamental Practice, just after you awake each morning. That way, you'll be continually imprinting the principles of breathing into your body and psyche without any distractions of motion or exercise, and you'll never drift far from a correct approach to breath work. The primary goal of the Fundamental Practice of Relaxed Breathing is to learn to breathe continuously and to be aware of our bodies as we do so.

As I describe the work, I'll remind you of how to apply the fundamental Principles of the Systema Breathing. These Seven Principles will apply to all the exercises presented in this book.

Natural Position

Standing upright is an excellent posture for the Fundamental Practice, but sitting or lying down are also acceptable positions.

Natural Body Position

Postural requirements for the standing practice are as follows

- Relaxed body – no tension at all
- Straight spine, level head
- Shoulders comfortably back and down
- Feet apart, about shoulder width
- Legs very slightly bent, but without tension
- Hands may hang down naturally at sides, or be placed on hips

When you stand in this way, we can say that you are keeping proper form, but what it really means is that you are in your normal and natural body position. This upright posture is very strong, and provides the perfect anatomical configuration for balanced movement in any direction, for martial arts, sports, and function in daily life. The natural position has a very close connection to correct breathing. The upright, balanced posture needs to be maintained by breathing alone, not by strength. Using deliberate muscular strength to uphold yourself you would not be relaxed.

When you are either over-tensed or unbalanced, or bent in any subtle way, or if your breathing becomes discontinuous, your natural position will *break* – that is, some sort of body bending, folding, or misalignment will occur – and then you can be easily manipulated by your partner. If, however, you continue to breathe calmly and steadily, in accordance with the principles that we'll introduce in this chapter, you will find yourself easily maintaining both strong natural position and an easy relaxation.

The requirement for relaxation applies particularly to your shoulder area – try to be aware of any residual tension there (which may cramp your breathing).

Begin all fundamental breathing practices by exhaling all residual air. Then, proceed to inhale fully and deeply. A full,

deep breath will involve no strain or excessive fullness – rather, it will feel "just right" and as though the air has thoroughly permeated your entire body *(Principle of Intake Sufficiency - pg. 45)*. As you inhale, be aware of how your breath may be "stuck" in a particular area of your body that is tense, tired, or ill.
For example, if your neck and shoulders are chronically tight, you may be able to feel or observe within yourself that the breath is not flowing freely through that area *(Principle of Non-Tension - pg. 49)*.

Try-It-Now!

Your natural position can be tested by a partner, who presses firmly in two opposite directions along your body's center line, or on two opposing sides of your body (shown in Figure 4-a). You try to maintain your natural standing position without tensing or bending.

1. For example, your partner might place one palm on the back of your head and another palm on your chest or abdomen, then press to see if you deform yourself in response.

2. Or, he might place one palm at the small of your back, and another on your forehead, then press firmly.

3. Or he might push from your sides, one palm pushing at your upper arm, while pushing with the other palm on your hip at the other side.

Try to stay relaxed and use your breathing to keep your shape during this drill!

As you inhale, softly gathering the air with your nose, be sensitive and attentive to the air's qualities. Also, inhale with every body part, so that you feel you are absorbing air from all over your body, not just your nose alone. As you begin to fill up, feel the air permeate the body, beyond the airway chambers of the nose, trachea, and lungs, and into all the deepest parts of the body. When you have practiced this way for some time, you will begin to truly feel that breathing is a deep physiological process rather than purely mechanical. This means that inhalation does not end at the lungs, and exhalation does not begin from the lungs.

Now, pause briefly as you terminate the inhale phase. Try to be aware of the natural cessation of "in-flow" as your body gets "just enough" air, and prepares for the next phase. Don't force, don't over-extend, and don't cut short *(Principle of the Pendulum - pg. 47; Principle of Continuity - pg 46)*. This natural pause is not a "hold."

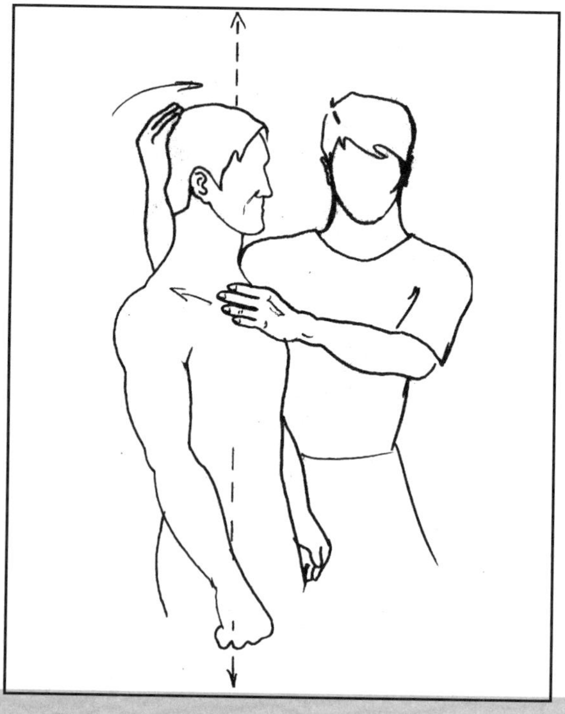

Figure 4-a: Form check with a partner

As you exhale, remember again that breathing is physiological, not mechanical. For now, you can understand that as a feeling of air leaving through the pores of the whole body, not just through the mouth. In later chapters, we will describe more complex variations of the outward breath phase that will greatly deepen your understanding and power, but for now just learn to feel the whole body exhaling smoothly.

How many times should you repeat the breath cycle?
Continue until you feel relaxed and your breathing is calm and even. You will begin to be aware of areas of breath blockage, which generally is a signal of tension, disease, pain, chronic injury, or fatigue. Just becoming aware of these "dead zones" is a big step toward restoring them to vitality.

As you inhale with our concept of "just enough" air *(Principle of Intake Sufficiency - pg. 45)*, you will find yourself relaxing. As you relax *(Principle of Non-Tension - pg. 49)*, your body loosens, and on the subsequent phases, you will find yourself inhaling more air, as a completely natural outcome of this practice. As this loosening unfolds, do not hold back, simply let your body take in the just the right amount of air for its present condition at each moment. As you learn to trust the process, with practice you will see that your body has its own intelligence. That means that once you have set the correct process in motion *(Principle of the Pendulum - pg. 47)*, you do not need to "interfere" with it in any way!

Starting Your Day

Your first use of the Fundamental Practice of Relaxed Breathing can be to start your day right. When we sleep, our vital signs (heart rate, blood pressure, respiration, and most other internal autonomic processes) slow quite a lot. If you leap out of bed immediately after opening your eyes each morning, you may stress your system unduly by presenting a sudden adaptive challenge, or shock, to the body. You are requiring it to move and function instantaneously. The body's efforts to adapt to the sudden demands of these "cold starts" can, over many years, have adverse health effects. People who suffer from any chronic health condition, such as high blood pressure or heart disease, need to be especially careful about this transition from rest to activity.

A better way to begin the day is with a breath-based warm-up routine. Again, the Seven Principles are the foundation for all the work described here.

After you first open your eyes in the morning, remain in your bed or sleeping place, reclining in a straight, natural posture, on your back, arms extended along your sides (Figure 4-b). This lying posture can also be used for regular breath practice at any time of day.

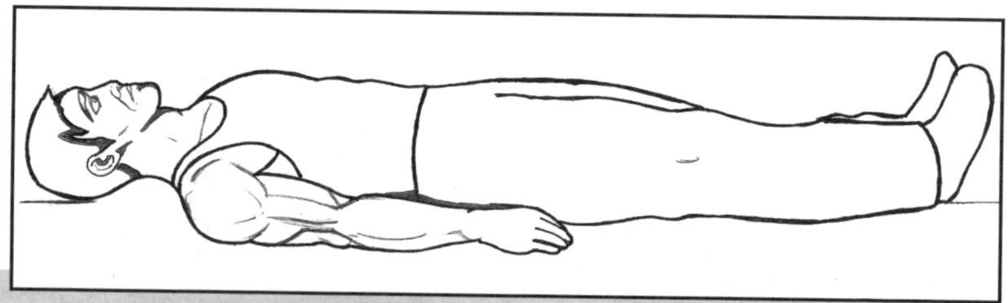

Figure 4-b: Lying down in a relaxed manner

Inhale sufficiently *(Principle of Sufficiency - pg. 45);* pause and hold the air in; then exhale, with all three phases of about equal duration. Repeat this a few times. Then, with your next inhalation, begin a wave-like tensing of every muscle in your body, beginning with your toes and feet, and extending the tension so that its maximum extension reaches your head and face. This tension does not have to be excessive (don't lock up your breathing), but you should be able to feel distinctly the muscular tension gradually moving up through each body part. Time your "wave" of tension so that its maximal extension reaches your head just as your "sufficient" inhale completes. Hold briefly and try to feel your pulse, throughout your body.

While holding your breath, be sensitive to the sensation of your own pulse. Your pulse originates from your heart's pumping of blood, but with practice your sensitivity will increase until you can feel a pulse in almost any body region. This sensitivity is the foundation of mastering your own autonomic processes. Russian monks and other holy persons have demonstrated this kind of self-mastery throughout history. In addition, this practice can increase your powers of psychological and spiritual observation. That increased awareness will be highly beneficial to yourself and others.

Then, begin to release the tension, again as a wave, but now reversing direction, sweeping down from the head and relaxing every body part in sequence down to your feet. This coordination of breathing cycles with a "wave" of alternating tension and relaxation is a typical feature of Systema Breathing.

Though the exercise involves muscular tension at certain moments, it is actually the prime vehicle for teaching you the *Principle of Non-Tension* *(Pg. 49)*. That's because **you can't control what you can't feel!** If you don't understand your tension thoroughly, and don't feel it when it arises, you can't control and develop a relaxation response. For the "warm-up" transition to upright, wakeful activity, it is sufficient to repeat this tension-relaxation cycle, tied to your inhale-exhale cycle, a few times before rising. You do this short morning routine until you feel toned and energized. This may vary based on how you feel that day, and based on your experience.

You can also work in the opposite mode – relax as you inhale, tense yourself as you exhale. Or, you can tense as you inhale, and maintain the tension while you exhale, for one or two cycles. These variations can help you to master the *Principle of Independence!* *(Pg. 48)*

For a nice finishing touch to this morning routine, after you have completed a few tension-relaxation cycles as described above, inhale once more, just sufficiently, and then hold your breath for as long as possible. We use breath holds as a special kind of training. In daily life, we constantly and repeatedly hold our breath unconsciously, which is generally harmful to the body and psyche, and blocks our physical work as well. However, it is a common unconscious habit. By holding our breath in training, we become familiar with the feeling of blocked breath, and this awareness is the first step to achieving conscious control over holding our breath. This holding work actually develops your understanding and control of the *Principle of Continuity! (Pg. 46)*

The practice of holding our breath also conditions our brain, heart and Nervous System to prevent the "panic" reaction that naturally accompanies prolonged holds. By resisting that panic, we develop our physical capacity for endurance and we strengthen our psyche to achieve difficult goals. Mastering this will help us to weather any kind of difficulty life may place before us.

So, when you train and feel the internal need and pressure to release your breath, struggle with yourself a little – extend the hold just a bit beyond where you would normally be comfortable. For these moments, as a panic reaction mounts, I have been told that both Vladimir and Mikhail pray to God. "Lord have mercy" is the simple and true prayer sufficient to cut you off from your earthly attachments and thus reduce fear. Try to remain calm, humble and controlled in your mind, even while struggling with this work.

The upcoming chapters of this book will introduce about a dozen specific breath methods or patterns. I'll also describe about a half dozen basic physical exercises. The most amazing feature of Systema Breathing is that pretty much any of the breath patterns can be applied to any of the basic physical exercises! There are hundreds of different ways and combinations for doing the most basic breath work.

However, even that smorgasbord is only a hint at the full richness of Systema Breathing. There are additional levels and even more advanced training possibilities. Everything begins with mastery of yourself, which can be accomplished through working on the methods and exercises presented in the upcoming chapters.

Chapter Five

The Core Work: Part 1

"In Systema Breathing, the body, mind and soul must all be present, functioning and connected. A lack in any one part greatly weakens the whole." – Mikhail Ryabko

The exercises described in this chapter, and the next, form the core of Systema Breathing. The four primary tools are **pushups**, **squats**, **leg raises**, and **situps**. This small group of simple exercises works on the three major muscle groups of the **upper body**, **mid-section**, and **legs**. They promote overall physical health and normalize your blood pressure and other body processes. This chapter introduces pushups and squats. The following chapter covers leg raises and situps.

You may think these are merely standard high school calisthenics. In Systema Breathing, they are far more. These exercises not only develop your breathing but, most importantly, connect breathing to physical activity. They form the link between breath principles and the physical and psychological challenges of real life. The exercises go beyond the physical, as they challenge you to overcome weakness and self-pity. By performing the work outlined here, you learn to conquer yourself.

In addition to the first exercises, the first set of breath patterns and methods are also presented here. A key feature of Systema Breathing is that the breathing patterns and counting styles can be applied to any kind of physical work – not only to the exercises of this chapter, or this book. While working on these exercises, always keep in mind the *Principles* of Systema Breathing (Chapter 3).

Basic Physiology

Cords or bands of connective tissue that bind a muscle to a bone and transmit muscular force are called tendons, and the ones that connect two bones in a joint or support your internal organs in place are called ligaments. Your tendons and ligaments have to be more resilient and tenacious than muscles. Though most physical regimens work for muscle development, the physical part of Systema Breathing is mainly concerned with strengthening tendons and ligaments. Your muscles will tire quickly under stress. But if you condition your tendons and ligaments, you can keep working long past the point of maximum muscle fatigue.

> **Listen-UP!**
>
> Endurance, longevity, and rejuvenating power lie within the *tendons.*

Pushups: Your Breath Pushes You

A *pushup* is any action of raising the entire length of your straight body from the floor primarily with arm motions. There are many variations, but the following fundamental points apply to almost any kind of proper pushup. The top line of your body is straight so that it would align to a wooden pole laid length-wise from your legs to the back of your head. Do not let your mid-section sag or hump, do not raise or lower your head, and do not let your knees sag. Support yourself with your hands, using either flat palms or fists. If you use fists, rest your weight on the whole surface of the knuckles and do not let your wrists bend inward or outward under pressure.

You may have your feet together, resting on the balls of the feet, or for a greater challenge you can cross your legs at the ankles, resting on the ball of one foot only.

Pushup Posture Basics

Body: Absolutely straight
Hands: Fists, or flat palms
Feet: Together, or crossed at ankles

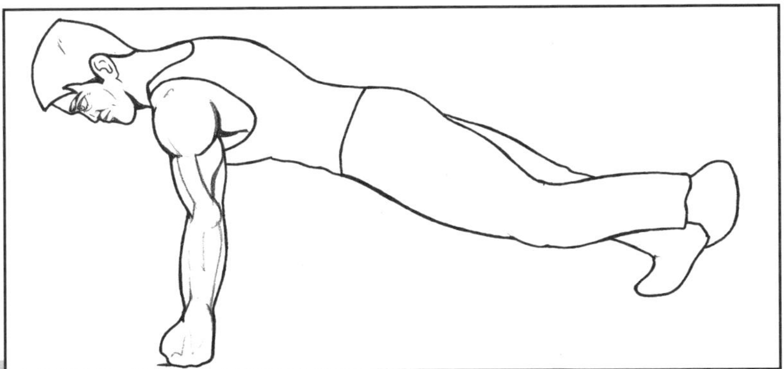

Figure 5-a: Pushup starting position

Lower yourself evenly, stopping just before your chest touches the floor. Rise uniformly and evenly, your whole body raising as a single unit, led by your breath action.

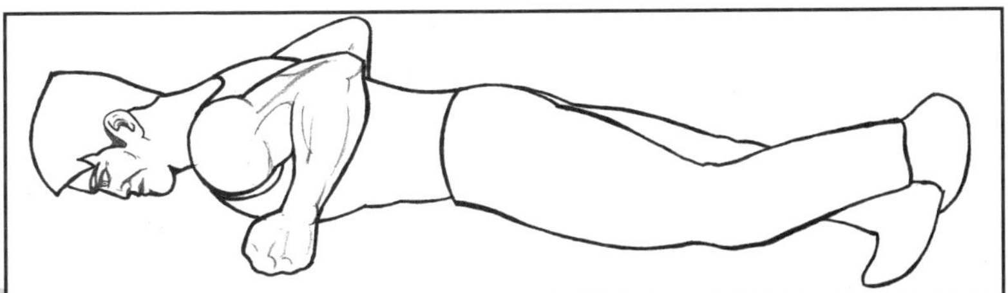

Figure 5-b: Pushup lowered position

While performing pushups, be sure to keep your face, neck, and shoulder muscles relaxed throughout the movement.

The Basic Full Breath Pattern

There are many ways to coordinate your breath with the pushup. Normally, you'd begin by exhaling the residual air completely in the start (raised) position (Figure 5-a), without moving. Then, the simplest breath pattern would be to inhale as you lower yourself, pause slightly at the bottom (Figure 5-b), then exhale as you rise. Remember to start the breath action (inhale or exhale) just a bit ahead of the physical motion, according to the *Principle of Leading.* You may also reverse it: exhale as you lower, and inhale as you rise.

The Halfway-Change Breath Pattern

You can change your breath halfway through an action. For pushups, you can begin in the raised position, and first exhale the residual air without movement. Then, begin to inhale just before you start to smoothly and slowly lower yourself (remembering the *Principle of Leading*). Continue to inhale smoothly until you are about halfway down. Then, calmly switch over to the exhale, while continuing to lower yourself smoothly, without any pause in your lowering motion. The exhale finishes just as you reach the fully lowered position. Begin your next inhale just before starting to rise, and finish the inhale as you reach the halfway point. Again, switch over to your exhale for the top half of the rise, back to the starting position, where your exhale finishes. Repeat for as many pushups as you can perform. The trick here is to maintain smooth, even, and continuous motion through the midway change of breath pattern (when you're halfway up or halfway down). Don't pause or change your speed in any way. You can also invert the pattern by beginning to lower with an exhale, switching to an inhale at midpoint, then symmetrically exhale and inhale on the rise.

Determination

Systema Breathing differs from other breath training systems, which try to make training comfortable. Here, you'll be confronted with reality-based physical and psychological challenges from the beginning. Your mind will initially tend to focus on the physical difficulty of the work.

Treat all the work described in this book as breathing exercises, rather than as physical or mechanical work. This will help your mind. You won't understand the miracle of breath until you push through your own limits.

Listen-UP!

Real progress comes with a psychological breakthrough – you learn to use your breath to mediate all physical effort.

In doing the exercises presented here and in the Core Work II (Chapter 6), you may come to a point of feeling very weak and shaky, and completely unable to continue. At these times, you should inhale through your nose, pulling the pain and fatigue out of your muscles and exhale it out of your mouth. You can also "grab" the pain and fatigue from your muscles with inhalation, and exhale it back out through the muscles. These inhales and exhales are done forcefully. The more discomfort you feel, the more intensely you need to breathe. This is described in more detail as "Burst Breathing" below.

Listen-UP!

Your breath's miracle power will be found only at your extreme limits.

Simply changing your breathing pattern can also help to overcome extreme fatigue. You will be able to keep your exercise going with the new pattern. This book offers many variations, so switch among them continuously, and you'll find a hidden reserve of new strength. This hidden reserve is tapped spontaneously in extreme situations by athletes, soldiers, and rescue workers. It is sometimes called the "Second Wind". Systema Breathing trains you to consciously control and extend that hidden power.

Stretch-your-Breath

In the Stretch-your-Breath Pattern, you align a *single extended breath action* to a *single movement*. Take a count of one to lower yourself all the way down, with a single smooth inhale and count 1 again for the rise with your exhale. As a variation, reverse and exhale for the count of one as you lower, then inhale for the count of one as you rise.

Next, count 1, 2 as you lower yourself smoothly (inhaling), and 1, 2 again as you rise (exhaling). Continue with a count of 1, 2, 3 as you lower, and 1, 2, 3 as you rise. Continue extending the count as long you can. You should follow the *Principle of Symmetry* in this training, so that after you reach your longest count sequence (for example, you might peak at 1, 2, 3, 4, 5, 6, 7 for the lowering action, and the same 7-count again for the rise). Then, you should reverse all the way back down: start by counting to 6 while lowering, 6 while rising, then 5 down and 5 up, 4 down and 4 up, etc., to finish with a single count of 1 for your final lower and 1 for your final rise. The important thing with stretched breath patterns is to make the physical motions slow and smooth, as one continuous movement, regardless of the counting stage, so that the longer and longer breath times coordinate perfectly with longer and longer physical actions (raising and lowering yourself).

Listen-UP!

When inhaling in the Stretch-Counted pattern, don't get greedy! Review the discussion of the *Principle of Sufficiency* (Chapter 3) for crucial points concerning how much to inhale on each movement.

The table below shows a possible Stretched Breath progression. Of course, it can be varied – for example, you could lower yourself on an exhale breath, instead of on an inhale as shown in the table. Or, you could go higher or lower than 7 as your longest count. It usually feels best to keep a kind of symmetry in your progression for this training. You should reverse downward from the peak (7 in the table), back through counts of 6, 5, 4, 3, 2, ending at 1 just as you began.

BREATH	**ACTION**	**COUNT**
Inhale	Lower	1
Exhale	Rise	1
Inhale	Lower	1 2
Exhale	Rise	1 2
•••	•••	•••
Inhale	Lower	1 2 3 4 5 6 7
Exhale	Rise	1 2 3 4 5 6 7
•••	•••	•••
Inhale	Lower	1 2
Exhale	Rise	1 2
Inhale	Lower	1
Exhale	Rise	1

Stretching your Breath - example pattern

Relaxation

As explained, with the *Principle of Non-Tension*, your muscles are not the target of this work. They should be only minimally involved. That means your body should be relaxed at all times. Remember that breath is our power source, and only a body free of excess tension allows for sufficiently deep breath.

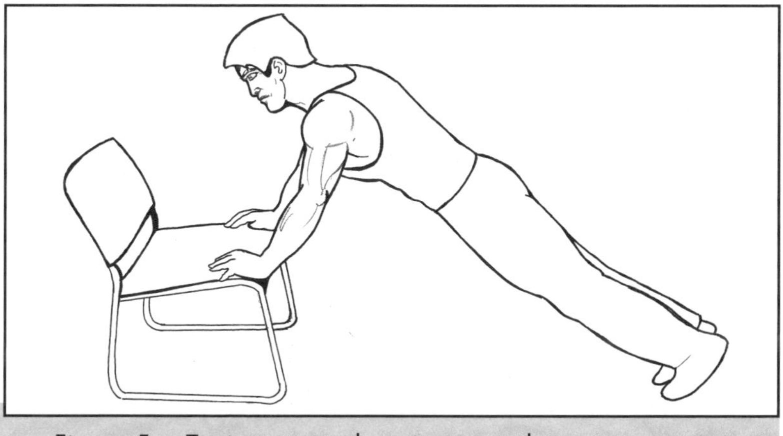

Figure 5-c: Testing your relaxation in pushups

Try-It-Now!

To check your relaxation in pushup position, try doing a few test pushups

1. At first, don't use the normal horizontal pushup position, on the floor. Try just a few with your hands resting on top of a low wall, a bench, or other low support. This places less demand on your upper body strength and helps you to feel your own degree of relaxation. Do a few pushups this way, with your body at 45-degree angle to the floor.
2. Try to relax your arms and shoulders to the greatest possible degree, while still accomplishing the work. That's the feeling of muscular relaxation that you should maintain while practicing all the exercises described in the book.

Even when doing pushups or the other hard work presented in these chapters, stay as relaxed as possible. In the beginning, you will need to check your own relaxation. Later, correct breathing itself will keep your body relaxed.

There's an important point that I'll mention now, for pushups, but I'll remind you in later sections as well, because it applies to all exercises.

Listen-UP!

You should always be breathing correctly – before, during and after the exercise.

You don't suddenly "turn on" correct breathing when you assume your perfect starting pushup position, and "turn it off" when you finish the final pushup of your session. Since pushups are a kind of floor work, remember your breathing even as you prepare to lower yourself to the floor, before you even attempt your first pushup. Breathe naturally, amply, with awareness, in through the nose and out through the mouth as you lower yourself before you start working. Then, after the final pushup, don't just tense up and jump up, forgetting your breath. Rise calmly and smoothly, with a relaxed body and full awareness of your natural breath.

Squats: Your Breath Raises You

A *squat* is lowering your upright body by bending your legs.

Squat Posture Basics

Body: Back straight throughout

Hands: Straight down in back of thighs

Feet: Shoulder width, heels flat, toes facing forward

Your back should remain upright throughout the lowering and rising motions, with your head and neck straight. Your hands should remain relaxed at your sides. Your feet are positioned facing forward about shoulder width apart, and your entire foot, including the heel, remains flat on the floor throughout the motion.

Listen-UP!

There may be a tendency to lean your upper body forward as you lower. Resist this tendency, and squat less deeply at first if necessary to maintain an upright back. Over time, you'll naturally learn to relax your hips to prevent this fault.

As with pushups, the *Principle of Leading* applies, so always let your breath action (inhale or exhale) begin just a little ahead of your physical motion (lower or rise). All the breath patterns introduced above for pushups can also be applied to squats. Proceed with the Basic Patterns, the Halfway-change Patterns, and the Stretch-your-Breath Patterns with squats as well as pushups. There are many additional patterns that can be used with Squats or any of the other exercises, which will be introduced in later chapters.

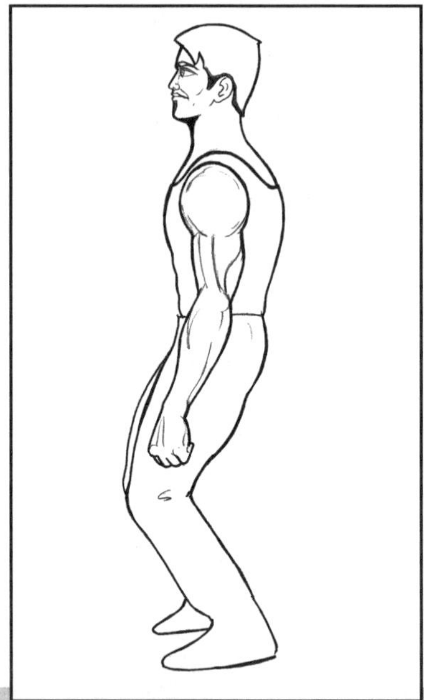

Figure 5-d: Squat in progress

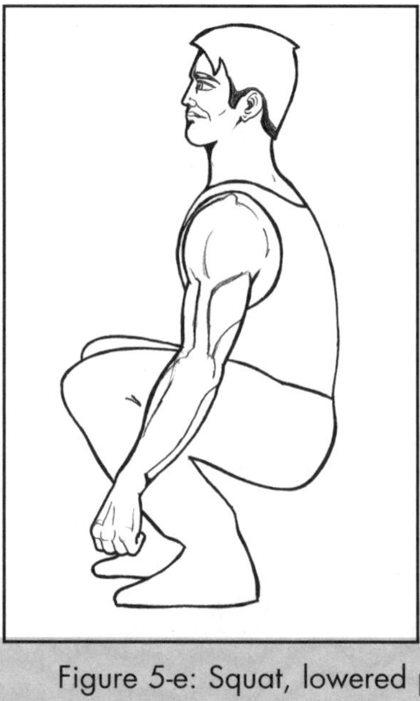

Figure 5-e: Squat, lowered position

Slow Motion

Here is a typically "fun" Systema Breathing practice! You can do just *one* squat (a single lowering followed by a single rise), but make it a little tough on yourself – do it *super slowly!* This can be controlled by a slow self-count or a timer. If you self-count, a good target is 20. Count from 1 and slowly begin to lower yourself... 2, 3, 4, 5, 6, 7, 8, 9, 10 - now you should be halfway down, don't pause - just keep lowering yourself slowly and smoothly ... 11, 12, 13, 14, 15, 16, 17, 18, 19, 20 - now you should be entirely down. In rising after a brief pause, follow the same principles. Begin again with 1, 2, 3, 4, 5, 6, 7, 8, 9, 10 - you should be halfway up now - 11, 12, 13, 14, 15, 16, 17, 18, 19, 20 – now you are standing all the way up again!

The key idea is to practice continuous motion – don't move in jerks, steps or increments. This work trains and refines your body sense and timing awareness. You want to reach the lowest point very naturally just as your smooth and slow count hits 20, with no rushing or stalling. It can be useful to have another person count for you. Try to conform your motions to his or her count. Maintain your smooth, even body motion throughout the count. Try this with a single squat as well. In order to do the slow motion exercises properly - this is what you need to learn:

Burst Breathing

The single squat to a count of 20 takes time to accomplish (with the Slow Motion breath pattern), and is quite strenuous. Burst Breathing is a perfect tool to handle this strain. If you begin to feel very tired, continue to breathe! You will have to perform many breath cycles during the slow lowering and rise. You should breathe using short, sharp impulses –

INHALE very shortly and sharply through your nose! Grab the pain and fatigue out of your muscles.

EXHALE very shortly and sharply through your mouth! Expel the pain and fatigue.

It sounds and feels like a rapid series of short puffs. Do this as fast as you need to, for overcoming your fatigue. The more pain and exhaustion you feel, the more intensely you need to breathe through it. Try this with a single v-e-r-y slow squat, or with a s-l-o-w version of any of the other exercises.

Listen-UP!

Psychologically, the slow work is probably the most challenging element of Systema Breathing. You are fighting yourself.

In fact, you have a perfect opportunity to fight your weaknesses, but "you" are still the ultimate winner of the contest, as long as you keep trying to learn from every experience. It is in working with these really difficult patterns, such as slow work, that the phrase "Don't feel sorry for yourself" is often heard in Russian Systema training. Hints for understanding the deepest meaning of this phrase are scattered throughout this book, and you may need multiple readings to understand it all. For now, if you are having trouble with the "slow work" on pushups, please review all of Chapter 4 (introducing the Fundamental Practice of Relaxed Breathing). Chapter 4 contains the purest essence of the Russian Systema, and has important hints on how to "overcome yourself".

Wall Squats

Begin with your back to the wall, feet shoulder-width apart and toes facing forward. Press your head, back, and legs smoothly to the wall surface. Then lower yourself in the basic squat position (as described and illustrated above) while trying to maintain contact with the wall (your head, back, buttocks). Make sure your heels are in contact with the wall and do not let your heels rise off the floor. As you lower, you can apply any of the breath patterns discussed previously. Basic breath patterns (as described above) are a good way to get familiar with wall squats. Exhale the residual air completely, then inhale as you lower, pause briefly, then exhale as you rise.

In another version, begin with your <u>face to the wall</u> as shown in Figure 5-f . Turn your head to one side and press your head, neck, shoulders, abdomen, hips, and legs as flush to the wall as you can. As you lower, try to maintain the contact as closely as possible. Your buttocks may tend to stick out, but try to minimize this as much as possible.

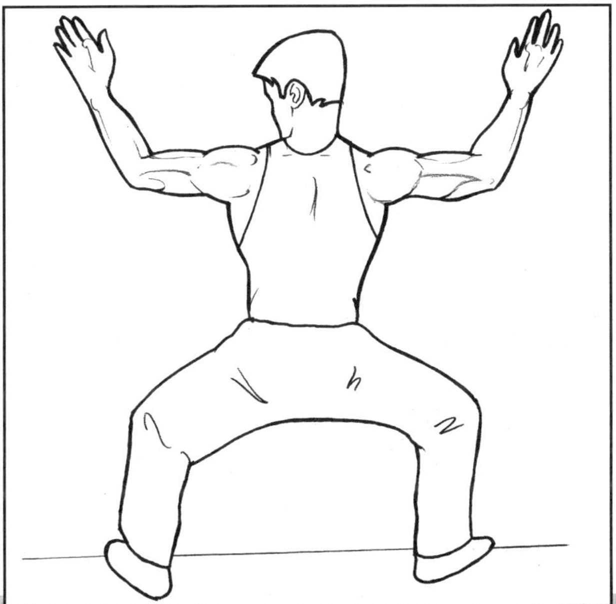

Figure 5-f: Wall-facing squat

In yet another flavor, the <u>side version</u>, you press the entire right side of your body, with your right arm raised, to the wall – including back of the shoulder, arm, hip, and leg. Keep your feet about shoulder width apart, and straight (Figure 5-g). As you lower, keep the contact with the wall while maintaining a straight back. Keep your heels on the floor all the time. You must also keep your buttocks tucked in, not protruding. Repeat the same movement with your left side against the wall.

After you've worked a bit with the basic squat motions, try the other breath patterns already introduced for pushups. That's the beauty of the Systema Breathing – <u>all</u> the breath patterns are intended to work with <u>any</u> of the exercises.

Figure 5-g: Wall squat, side version, lowered position

Listen-UP!

All the breathing patterns introduced so far, including those for pushups, can be applied to any of the wall squat positions!

Bundled Breath Pattern

In the Bundled Breath Pattern, a single breath action covers or bundles together multiple movements. It can be applied to any of the exercises (pushups, squats, etc). Start with a single squat. Begin to inhale and squat all the way down. Then continue this inhale and rise. In other words, your single inhale has extended throughout the complete squat. Then, do another squat, this time stretching your exhale to cover both the lowering and the rising. Don't rush the physical motions! Just align a single, long, and calm breath action (inhale or exhale) with the complete squat cycle (lowering, raising).

When you can do this calmly and smoothly, try doing two full squats (lower/raise once; lower/raise again), but all accomplished on a single, extended inhale breath action! Then, do two complete squats with a single, long smooth exhale. See how far you can go with this, how many good, precisely executed squats you can do on a single breath action. Maybe three, maybe more?

The table below shows a starting set, up to three complete squats per each breath action. The "Pause / Hold" means that you can optionally do a complete squat while holding your breath. More will be explained about breath holds as an exercise element in Chapter 6. It is fine to do the sets without the "Pause / Hold" phase between the "Inhale" and "Exhale" phases.

BREATH PHASE	NUMBER OF COMPLETE SQUATS (LOWER, RAISE)
Single Inhale	1
Pause / Hold	1
Single Exhale	1
Single Inhale	1, 2
Pause / Hold	1, 2
Single Exhale	1, 2
Single Inhale	1, 2, 3
Pause / Hold	1, 2, 3
Single Exhale	1, 2, 3

Buddy Work

With many of the Systema Breathing Exercises, you can work with a partner to achieve greater sensitivity and have more fun. Pushups and squats lend themselves particularly well to partner work.

Partner Synchrony & Mirroring

A feeling of fellowship pervades Russia's traditional culture. That sense of community is reflected all the way into Systema Breathing. Even though the Core Work so far has been presented as individual exercises, it can and should be done with a partner as often as possible. For example, you can do pushups with a partner by lining up alongside one another. You can touch arms or shoulders lightly to assure perfect coordination. For squats, you can work facing, side-to-side, or back-to-back.

One partner can lead and the other follows, trying to mimic not only the gross physical movements of the leader, but his breathing as well. This can be done to a pre-set count such as 5 or 10, or be freely paced by the leader. The job of the passive partner is to mimic precisely the actions of the leader. The leader should be creative – he doesn't have to simply lower and raise himself. The leader can go halfway and then rise, can vary the speed, can re-position his hands or feet – anything goes! The trick for the follower is to try to "ape" as many nuances of the leader as possible, beyond gross posture. Keep the same rhythm, the same breath pattern, the same posture – even the same spirit and feeling. Mirroring can be done with any of the Core Work practices.

Listen-UP!

The benefits of working with a partner include:

- Increased endurance – observing somebody else takes you outside yourself, lessens your self-indulgence and attention to yourself, so you don't give up as easily
- Improved observational skills
- Increased ability to respond flexibly to a changing situation under stress

A good way to begin is to have your partner do five good pushups, with breathing (any of the patterns given in this chapter) while you attempt to replicate both his breath pattern and his motions. Then, switch so that you are the controlling partner.

With pushups, this can be done side-by-side (touching) or head-to-head.

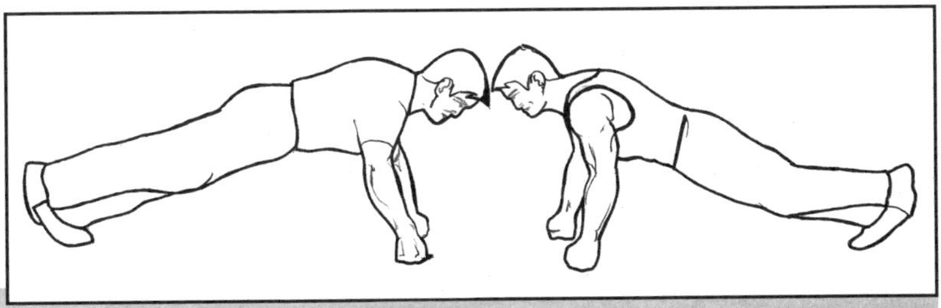

Figure 5-h: Pushups with a partner

The side-by-side version is particularly fun, as you can place a tennis ball between your shoulders, for automatic alignment checking. Make sure that in this case your elbows are facing back.

For squats, you can do partner work facing one another, or side-to-side, or back-to-back.

Keep in mind that you are attempting to mirror or copy as much of your partner's motion as you can – including, most particularly, being sensitive to his breathing.

Try to remember what's in this chapter, because as you proceed through the book, new exercises will be introduced, with new breathing patterns, which can be varied by going back to the basic breath patterns introduced here.

Figure 5-i: Squats with a partner, back-to-back

Chapter Six

The Core Work: Part 2

Sit-ups: Your Breath Pulls You

Sit-ups are another way to work with the connection between your body and psyche, mediated via your breath. This connection becomes no longer a mystery to you, it becomes more tangible. Yet, you start to open up another mystery – you begin to understand yourself.

In a sit-up, you lie on the floor, on your back, and then raise your upper body. The upper body must be raised to ninety degrees, and sometimes farther.

Sit-Up Posture Basics

Body: Lie relaxed, flat on your back, head straight

Arms: Arms extended along your sides, straight and relaxed

Legs: Keep legs flat, straight, comfortable with feet on the floor throughout all movement

The key element in Ryabko-style breathwork sit-ups is that your upper body rises as a single unit or a single straight piece. Your upper body should conform to a perfect straight line, from your head to your waist, in both raising and lowering. No bending! In other words, during and at finish of the rise phase, your body should be straight and you'll look like the letter 'L', never the letter 'C'.

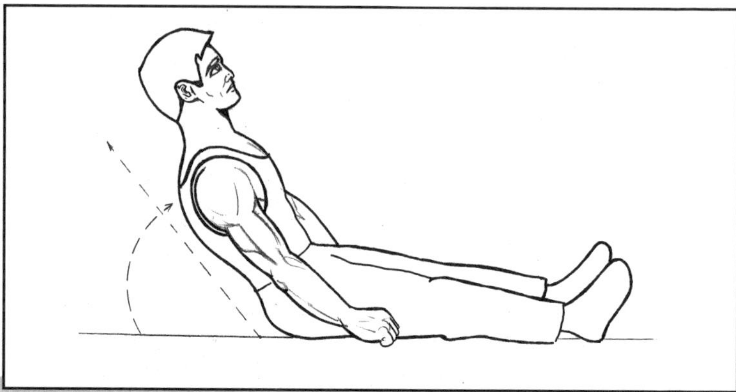

Figure 6-a: Sit-up, midway position

It is particularly important that your (straight) legs do not rise during your upper body's lift. It may seem difficult to keep your legs flush to the floor, but if you are truly relaxed, truly "pulling" with the breath alone, not levering via body mechanics, you will be amazed – your legs will stay flat and comfortable as you lift yourself!

Listen-UP!

Make sure that you do not arch your lower back – this would strain the lumbar spine joints.

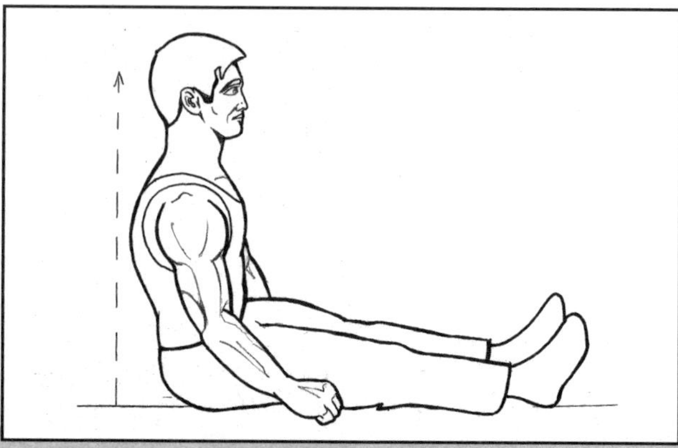

Figure 6-b: Sit-up, upright position

For breathwork, you need not go past the 90-degree upright position shown in Figure 6-b. If you want to work on stretching, you can extend past 90 degrees at the end of your rise, to lean forward along your legs as much as possible. But even when you are adding the stretching phase, control and align your entire rise with your breath. That means that even if you extend past ninety degrees, your rise finishes with your breath action (the inhale or exhale).

As for breathing, you can use all the patterns introduced so far, everything from the Core Work, Part 1. For example, rise as you inhale, lower as you exhale, or try reversing that (Basic Breath Pattern). Rise halfway as you inhale, continue to rise and finish with exhale, then inhale as you begin to lower, smoothly switch to exhale as you get halfway down (Halfway-Change Breath Pattern). You can also use the Stretched Breath Pattern, Slow Motion Breath Pattern, and the Long Inhale and Long Exhale, all from the Core Work, Part 1.

Now let's go through some other creative variations.

Burst Breathing with Static "midway" Positions

You can hold yourself statically in a mid-point position, or anywhere in the range from highest to lowest position. While holding still in the position, you can practice the Burst Breathing (short, sharp breathing as described in Chapter 5, Core Work Part 1). For push ups, squats, leg raises and sit-ups, a good holding position is the 45 degrees (midway). It is the most difficult point in the range to hold, as the muscles are in a disadvantageous position to contract and you have to use tendons. Try to relax as much as possible and inhale any pain, tension, or fatigue from the tensed area, and exhale it straight out of your body. This can be done using the "Burst Breathing" introduced in the Core Work, Part 1. Keep yourself relaxed. With a bit of experience, you'll be able to hold for an extended period.

In holding a pushup, you could also use the midway position or the fully raised upright position. Your arms could either be out from your body at 45 degrees, or tucked close.

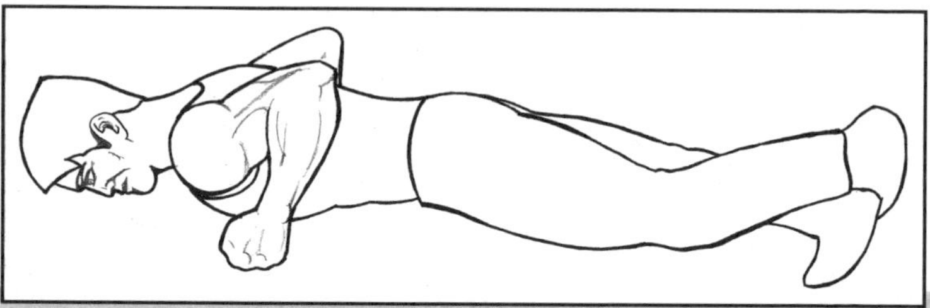

Figure 6-c: Pushup, midway hold position

Leg Lifts: Your Breath Lifts You

Leg lifts require you to lift your straight legs while lying flat on your back.

Leg Raise Posture Basics

Body: Flat on your back, head looking straight up
Arms: Extend straight alongside your body
Hands: Can be tucked under your buttocks for support if needed

Your upper body should remain relaxed at all times. Keep your entire back pressed flat along the floor. Your legs are kept straight, without any bending, as they rise. Most people can raise their straight legs to at least a 90-degree angle (straight up) without too much tension.

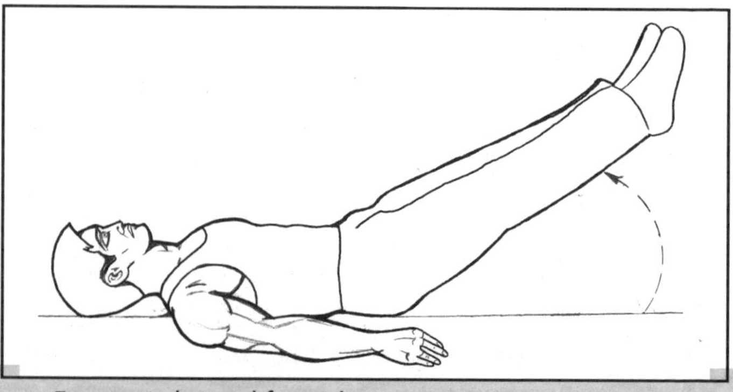

Figure 6-d: Leg lift, midway position

With practice, many people are able to fold their straight legs entirely back up over their heads and touch the floor behind with their toes. In the beginning, you may wish to raise to only 90 degrees (legs straight up). You can work gradually toward the full "heels over head" extension!

Figure 6-e: Leg lift, fully extended position

Listen-UP!

It is very important that you watch the position of your lower back during the Leg Lifts. If your abdominal muscles are weak, as your legs are elevated or lowered though the range of zero to about 45 degrees your lower back will be arching and actually coming off the floor. In this case, the weight of your legs will be carried by the ligaments and joints of your lower spine rather than by your muscles and that may lead to trauma of the lower spine. Make sure that your lower back is in full and firm contact with the floor while you go through this challenging range. In fact, you should have "the ant-crawl-contact" – lower back pressed against the floor so tightly that not a single ant would be able to crawl between your lower back and the floor. If you cannot keep your back tightly pressed to the floor, the easy solution is to support your pelvis with your hands between your buttocks and the floor. (In case you still cannot do it properly you may need a period of some gentle abdominal strengthening before proceeding with the Sit Ups and Leg Lifts.)

Leg Raises Offer a Special Breath Capacity Test

Leg raises are especially helpful in understanding some fine points of Systema Breathing. Try a few leg raises, raising on your inhale, but cease your leg motion immediately when your inhale reaches the point of perfect sufficiency. Don't cheat by allowing your legs' momentum to carry them past your point of breath fullness. Even if your inhalation is complete but your have not reached the 90-degree midpoint - stop, lower your legs, and repeat. Respect the *Principle of Sufficiency*.

Over time, this introductory practice will teach you sensitivity to the breath/body coordination, and will slowly tend to expand your relaxation. Your state of natural fullness will also increase in capacity. Eventually, you will find that as your breath reaches a naturally full state, your legs are ending up farther and farther past the 90-degree midpoint – stopping their rise just when the stage of natural inhale sufficiency is reached.

Use leg lifts as an aid in learning not to inhale to the point where you create tension on your internal organs and shoulders. When you approach that point of tension, you stop - that is all the air you need. No excess tension, but maximum air intake.

Holding your Breath

The great thing about this work is that you can apply all the breath patterns introduced in Chapter 5 for pushups and squats to the leg raises. But we haven't finished trotting out the variety of patterns in Systema Breathing – not by a long shot.

One interesting training drill is to deliberately hold your breath. This is not the unconscious holding that we all do when we are concentrating, or get tense, tired, or overly emotional. Instead, it's a deliberate method of conditioning our bodies and minds to overcome adversity – similar to what we introduced in Chapter 4 for the Fundamental Practice. But now, it's going to be even more interesting as we perform work while holding.

For leg raises (or any of the four basic exercises) you can begin with either a complete and sufficient inhale or exhale. Then hold your breath and perform 5 to 10 relaxed, even, and smooth leg raises, while holding your breath. You can also begin with 5 to 10 leg raises using the Basic Breathing Pattern, or one of the others, and finish with 5 to 10 repetitions while holding your breath.

From a superficial viewpoint, holding the breath appears to contradict the *Principle of Continuity*. But physiologically, your respiration never completely stops. The exchange of oxygen for carbon dioxide, or vice-versa, continues internally. So physiologically, the hold is just an extension of an ordinary breath phase (inhale or exhale).

Holding is used in Systema Breathing to train the psyche. When the breath is held, the organs, including the heart and brain, begin to experience oxygen starvation. In an untrained person, this leads to a panic reaction. Even the panic reaction requires energy to maintain itself, which simply worsens the oxygen starvation! With systematic training over a prolonged period, the natural panic reaction can be overcome. On deeper and deeper levels, the threshold of panic onset will be pushed further and further away.

The purpose of prolonged breath holds in training is to condition you not to switch into the panic state in a real emergency, such as prolonged underwater submersion or when gas fumes have poisoned the air. In defensive applications, it is essential to avoid panic reactions when experiencing a sudden act of violence, such as a hand over the mouth from the back. With training the panic reaction can be avoided, and the existing air will be more than sufficient to allow an effective counterattack. Familiarity with the breath hold condition leads the body to delay and minimize its panic response. In a real emergency, the conditioning will allow your body to make more efficient use of any remaining oxygen to take practical steps for saving yourself or others. The panic reaction may still occur, but it will be much less intense than in an untrained person, because the oxygen-deprived state has become a common and familiar state for your body.

Free Style

We've covered a variety of patterns, structures, and counting methods. It is often good to throw all that overboard and work freely to find your own limits. See how strong and disciplined you are and test yourself by starting a series of infinite pushups or squats. When you get exhausted, use "Burst Breathing" or any other change of breath pattern to keep going. Sometimes even suddenly holding your breath can give you strength to continue! When you are truly exhausted and feel you cannot continue, just try to do one more... or three more...

If you approach the work as first and foremost a breathing exercise, rather than physical conditioning, there ought to be no limit - just as there is no pre-set limit to how long you can sit comfortably breathing in an easy chair! When you finish your work, if you've done the exercises properly, you'll feel a positive fatigue rather than absolute exhaustion physically and will feel refreshed mentally.

Chapter Seven

Hit the Road!

"And thou shalt show them the way wherein they must walk, and the work that they must do." - Exodus18;20

One of the main ideas of Systema Breathing is the idea of pacing. We want to adapt our breathing to the level of effort and stress with the ultimate goal of breathing in the same even, calm, full style both before working, during work, at the peak of work, when finishing, and when back at rest. Walking and running practice offers an ideal "laboratory" to work with our pacing and control. Our goal will be to let our breath pace us as we walk or run.

Walking

Start your inhale slowly walking in a normal posture, and stay relaxed. To coordinate breathing, begin with a simple pattern of 1-step per every complete inhale, and 1-step for your complete exhale. Try to keep a precise alignment of steps with breath cycles. This might feel a bit robotic at first, but just relax, loosen up, take natural steps and start enjoying yourself: 1-step-inhale; 1-step-exhale; 1-step-inhale; 1-step-exhale, …, etc. Count your steps as you go.

Then move to 2-steps for inhale (one single, smooth inhale continuously over 2 steps), followed by 2-steps for exhale (a single, smooth exhale distributed over 2 steps). If your training area is small, you may wish to walk in a circle for the work described in this section. After a few circles, move up to 3-steps per (single, continuous) inhale, 3-steps per exhale. After a few circles at 3-count, you may then move on smoothly to 4, 5, 6, up to 7 steps or more. At each count, try to do approximately the same number of circles, for symmetry. Naturally, you will begin to step somewhat quicker on the higher breath counts, but try to stay relaxed, even, and calm-minded throughout. It is also possible to perform the same patterns with a light jog or run. After reaching your peak count (for example, 8-steps per inhale action, 8-steps per exhale action), you should wind back down sequentially to 7-steps, 6, etc. until you finish with 1-step per inhale, 1-step per exhale. This kind of slow buildup to a peak intensity, followed by working gradually back down to the starting point is called a pyramid sequence.

After performing an entire pyramid sequence this way, you will feel highly energized and, if you have followed all instructions, your breathing will be completely calm, settled and natural.

When you feel comfortable with the basic pyramid pattern above, you can try more challenging variations. These variations require excellent concentration. When done correctly they offer a strong psychological and physical benefit. One variation is a triangle sequence of three breath phases: inhale, hold, exhale (one step in each phase). Or the more challenging square sequence: inhale, hold, exhale, hold (one step in each phase). When you are comfortable with this, you can add further variety by changing the number of steps in each phase as shown below:

5 steps inhale, 3 steps hold, 5 steps exhale
3 steps inhale, 5 steps hold, 3 steps exhale
2 steps inhale, 4 steps hold, 2 steps exhale
5 steps inhale, 3 steps hold, 2 steps exhale
1 step inhale, 3 steps exhale
3 step inhale, 1 steps exhale

You can further challenge your concentration by placing obstacles in your path, or asking a partner to use a stick to impede you on every circle. You will need to jump over or duck under these obstacles as you walk. Try to maintain an even rhythm of constant breathing no matter what obstacles you encounter.

Running

The same approach can be taken to running. Begin with a relaxed jog at 1-step-inhale, 1-step-exhale as above. Continue to increase the number of steps-per-breath-phase, until you reach a peak of 8 or 9 running steps, or the most you can handle. Some highly trained adepts in Systema Breathing can work at paces of up to 20 steps-per-breath-phase! Whatever your personal peak, remember to scale back down from it according to the Principle of Symmetry (use a pyramid sequence as described above), and end at 1 step-per-breath-phase, just as you began.

Applying symmetry to runs over long distances will require you to estimate your midpoints (in either time or distance as appropriate to your purpose and situation) and scale the buildup and wind-down from that.

The two amazing things about this work are that:

a) it will enable you to run indefinitely, over incredible distances, without fatigue (as long as you maintain your counting and step/breath alignment over the entire distance)

b) when you finally finish, your breath will be calm, full and normal – none of the usual gasping and grabbing for air like a beached fish.

The running can be further enlivened with special circuits (assuming you are running in a circular pattern). This can involve particular breath conditions, e.g. holding the breath as discussed in the Core Work, Part 2. You can pick a spot on your circuit, and begin to hold as you pass that spot. Try to maintain the hold all the way around the circuit, and don't release until you pass that spot again. Try holding for two circuits, or more! Then continue with your previous pattern, wherever you suspended the pyramid count. Another way to add some spice to this work is by occasionally rolling through a step. Rolls are presented in detail in the next section.

Rolls

It may seem surprising that rolls are included in Systema Breathing. Rolling is not usually a feature of breath training programs. We all have had incidents of slipping, tripping or being pushed. Knowing how to fall without injuring yourself is of great value to any person. The chances of injuries are decreased dramatically with some practice of rolling. Moreover, if you know how to roll, your fear of falling is drastically reduced – and this makes you less tense in general during walking, running, playing any sport, carrying a child and so on.

Rolls present a great opportunity to practice breathing while the body is not in its standard positions and help you master *Breath Independence* (Chapter 3). Another reason for introducing rolls, (and training with the ground and walls), is the close association of breathwork with martial arts and survival applications. In martial arts, training in rolls is an integral part of preparation for ground fighting. Rolls are useful in both defense (evasion and escape) and attack (closing the gap; surprise use of legs; etc.) Although martial arts applications are outside the scope of this book, we find that in Systema Breathing, roll training also reinforces these concepts and principles. Rolling is one of the training methods that should be practiced to make you not only a superior fighter, but a better, healthier and calmer person.

All the principles of Systema Breathing apply to rolls. The dynamic nature of rolls tends to emphasize the importance of some basic ideas of Systema overall. The first principle for roll training is relaxation. You must learn not to "hold yourself" as you approach the floor. You must learn to surrender to the motion, and relax downward smoothly into the floor. Because a calm, quiet, and relaxed roll, at full speed, is a skill that can take time to develop,

Systema Breathing provides a number of gentler, graded practice methods that provide the same physical and psychological benefits as the "commando" roll training of combat arts, or the break-falls of martial sports.

Physically, relaxation requires a dynamic balance point. You can't collapse to the floor in a heap, but you can't tense up either. You need to establish the minimal effective control of each body part as it contacts the surface. The other physical basics include never rolling directly onto the head, neck, or spine. The body contact surface is always a broad, flat muscle plane such as back of the shoulders, side of back, side of hip, buttocks and thighs.

Psychologically, relaxation implies absence of fear. Fear causes physical tension and distorted perception, both of which can lead to damage in rolls. For some people, rolling can be scary, and furthermore, in the Russian Systema training, it can be even more challenging because mats are discouraged! This can be shocking to people from other arts, but in the Russian Systema we feel that mats condition you to have less respect for the ground. You may develop habits of excess tension without realizing it. We sometimes say that "a mat on the floor for training is like a person who lies to you. The hard floor is an honest friend, that won't lie. It will always point out your mistakes."

Energetically, relaxation implies control of breath during all phases of motion. A roll should be soft, with no sound heard apart from the smooth flow of breath. Rolls may be practiced in any portion of the breath cycle, as long as control is exercised.

The principles above raise rolling practice from a tedious training necessity to a fundamental energy-charging regime in its own right. The actual tactics and styles of Systema rolling are infinite. The training methods described here are the three basic practices most suited to beginning work in breath cultivation. Systema rolling practice encompasses much more than this chapter can treat fully.

A. Knee Front Roll

Begin this basic trainer move by kneeling on the floor. Relax and exhale as you bend forward. Extend one (or both) arms out fully to your sides as you tuck your head to one side, nearing the floor. Slowly, gently, with full attention to smooth breathing, roll your shoulder, then side of back, over onto the floor in front, forming a diagonal contact line, from initial shoulder, across spine, to opposite lower back/hip. Gently repeat, multiple times.

Figure 7-a: Front roll from knees

B. Back Roll – from sitting on your buttocks.

The relaxed back roll may be initiated from sitting or standing position. It begins as your buttocks contact the floor. Roll backward gently, exhaling, relaxed. Tuck your head to one side, and curl softly. As you finish the roll, rather than ending cramped and curled on your knees, extend your legs completely, as though you are a thick Oriental carpet being unrolled fully. You end fully flat facing down on the floor. The practice of leg raises, as described in Chapter 6, prepares you for doing back rolls correctly.

C. Standing Front Roll

Similar to A (knee roll) but now begin from standing posture. Lower your upper body, extend one leg backwards, and extend the arm on that same side fully outward. As your shoulder on that extended side begins to approach the floor, tuck your head and roll softly forward. There should be no sound but your breath as you roll on through.

Figure 7-b: Front roll from standing

With these three basic rolling skills mastered, you can begin to work on sustained series of continuous rolls, with attention to breathing.

Roll Sequences for Breath Training

You may wish to practice a simple series of the same type of roll, one after another in a single stream from one end of your practice area to the other and back again. In doing a roll series of this kind, you can experiment with different breathing patterns. It often feels very natural to exhale through the roll. This tends to promote even, relaxed movement. When exhaling through the roll, there should be no interruptions, holding, or any form of discontinuity in your breath. Here's where Audible Breathing, the supplementary advice introduced in Chapter 3, really applies. With audible exhalation throughout a roll, you or your partner should be able to diagnose any blockage, tension, or discontinuity in motion, as those problems will manifest in the breath. Your body should make no other noise throughout the roll motion, other than your audible exhalation.

In addition to rolling on the exhale, you should experiment with rolls that finish in any stage of the breath cycle. Learn to roll on inhale, on exhale or on hold. This is another drill on making breathing independent of your actions and body position – the *Principle of Independence*.

You can also try inhaling, or even the special practice of Holding your Breath through a roll. The point is not to find the single perfect breathing pattern for every conceivable roll, in every conceivable situation. The point is to achieve conscious mastery and have the power to choose and adapt your breathing and motion to any situation. In addition to performing single rolls with a single breath action, you can perform a sequence of rolls with a single breath action. For example, you can perform a standing front roll as you begin to exhale. As you come out of the initial roll, now down on the floor, continue with further rolls, from kneeling or lying positions, as long as you can continuously exhale. When you can no longer continuously exhale, stand up and inhale, simultaneously.

Also, rather than just practice a continuous series of rolls, you can intersperse occasional rolls within a longer series of other movements from Systema Breathing. For example, the circular patterns of walking and running, described in this chapter, can be amped up by "sprinkling" some rolls in, once in a while. If a training partner is directing the pace and count, he may want to occasionally signal that a front roll should be done whenever he claps. Similarly, a partner can signal you to turn and perform a quick back roll, after which you continue in your original walking or running direction. If you have no partners, you can still intersperse occasional rolls into your walking and running routines, whenever you feel like it. You can also place obstacles in your roll path or work with dynamic barriers such as a partner using a long stick to impede you, as described in Chapter 6. As in the walking and running practice, try to maintain a calm, even, and controlled breath pattern at all times.

Chapter Eight

Relaxation and Tension Methods

"Who hath put wisdom in the inward parts? Or who hath given understanding to the heart?" - Job 38;12

Earlier chapters had you doing pushups, squats, sit-ups, and leg raises. We've also gotten you walking, running, and rolling. Now it's time for something maybe a bit less physically strenuous, but equally important and challenging. As you learn the work introduced here, reflect back on the material from the earlier chapters. The work introduced in this chapter will deepen your overall understanding.

Relaxation is a pre-condition of correct breathing, as emphasized in the Seven Principles of Systema Breathing (Chapter 3). But exactly how can we relax? Most of us carry unnecessary tension in our bodies, yet it doesn't help much when teachers admonish us "Relax! Right now! You're still too tense!" Somehow that kind of coaching clutches us up even more. We need to learn how to relax.

Systema Breathing includes specific exercises that can rid us of the excess baggage of unconscious, non-functional tension. That extra tension causes us to tire more easily in physical work, and hampers our freedom of movement. Excess tension can also affect us psychologically, causing us to give up too early when things get tough.

You can't eliminate something if you aren't even aware of it. The methods introduced in this chapter will help you to identify excess tension and then release it. This work also creates a more intimate awareness of your body's internal states. Also, the breath training introduced in this book has different effects depending on how relaxed you are. The more you can control your own internal state, the greater the results you can harvest from your practice.

This chapter introduces patterned alternations of whole-body or body-part tension and relaxation, coordinated with breathing. We deliberately create tension in specific focus areas (such as legs, arms, abdomen, neck, etc.) and then consciously relax the focus area(s). This is how we learn to control our bodies and to consciously detect the difference between tension and relaxation. With each cycle of breath, whenever we relax the controlled tension in a body part or the whole body, the resulting relaxation is slightly deeper, or more complete, than before. Also, when the local tension is created, we learn to tell the difference between the tensed focus area and the rest of the body, which must remain completely relaxed. This training also brings increased control over your body and freedom of movement.

Freedom is the ability to move each body part independently of the rest. Once in class, I had just observed Vladimir perform yet another jaw-dropping combative stunt while sparring, such as throwing his opponent with his chin, or instantly kicking the knife from the hand of a fast slashing attacker, or immovably clamping the fist of someone attacking from behind between his shoulder blades. I felt puzzled. I had never observed Vlad doing much, or anything along the lines of classical martial arts stretching and warm-ups, with a support rail and the splits and so on. Yet he seemed more flexible to me than any Olympic gymnast, ballet dancer or yoga teacher I'd ever seen. When I asked him about this seeming contradiction, he smiled mysteriously and replied: "No, I'm not flexible. I'm free." That kind of practical freedom is developed by the work introduced in this chapter.

Whole-Body 'Wave' Tension Exercises

You can perform the wave tension practice either standing (in a natural upright position, as described in Chapter 4, The Fundamental Practice of Relaxed Breathing), or lying down on your back, with your arms relaxed by your sides.

In wave tension practice, we begin by inhaling as we tense the body from the head down to the feet. Starting with your scalp, tense your face, jaw, neck, shoulders, arms, hands, chest, abdomen, back, buttocks, thighs, knees, calves, right down through your ankles to your toes. That means, on completion of the inhale, the entire body is as tense as possible (every muscle, every area). The tensing is completed at the feet, just as the inhale finishes. Pause and hold the breath and the tension briefly. Then, on the exhale, reverse the direction of the relaxation wave, now moving from the feet to the head. This wave principle can also be applied in reverse, i.e. starting from the feet and moving to the head, on the inhale, then hold and exhale while relaxing from the head down to the feet.

After several passes of 'wave' breathing as described, you may want to try the 'quick freeze' version. In this variation, you inhale quickly and sharply, while simultaneously tensing every muscle in the body - not in a sweep or wave pattern as above, but all at once. Pause while maintaining the tension. Then exhale and relax completely, again all at once. When you have fully exhaled, relax completely and lie quietly, or perform another cycle. You can also reverse this quick freeze practice, meaning that you exhale sharply while simultaneously tensing everything, and then inhale as you relax.

When you have got a good understanding of this work and a good feel for it, you can try it with lighter degrees of tension. Try it with one-half your full tension, then one quarter tension and so on. But even though you can learn to tense up to a lesser degree, you must always maintain a clear distinction between the tensed and the relaxed state in practice.

We have been taught that when you understand this work perfectly you can instantly "tense up" only your Nervous System, that is, your nerves alone, without any obvious muscular tension at all! And then you'll learn the contrast to that, which is complete relaxation of your entire nervous system. That's how sensitive you may become if you persist in this work.

'Segmented' Tension Exercises

In segmented tension practice, we specifically tense one body area while inhaling – leaving all the rest of the body (everything outside the tensed target zone), completely relaxed. This is easy to say but very hard to achieve. It's an interesting training challenge! Normally this is practiced while lying on your back, as with the wave tension work described above. You may also attempt this while standing upright in the natural position.

Using your mind together with your body, inhale into the target areas listed below as you tense each one up. Beginners can work very well with this list, but at more advanced stages, any body area is a potential candidate zone, though some areas of the body may require special additional training methods. Work beyond this basic list should be carried out under the personal supervision of a qualified Systema Breathing instructor. All tension is performed during the inhale phase for this basic training level.

<u>Light tension over entire body;</u> pause; exhale; relax completely.
<u>Strong tension over entire body;</u> pause; exhale; relax completely.
<u>Both legs;</u> pause; exhale; relax completely.
<u>Both arms;</u> pause; exhale; relax completely.
<u>Stomach area;</u> pause; exhale; relax completely.
<u>Back;</u> pause; exhale; relax completely.
<u>Chest;</u> pause; exhale; relax completely.
<u>Neck;</u> pause; exhale; relax completely.

When you feel you understand how to tense a small local area, such as your abdomen alone, while thoroughly relaxing all the rest of your body (including the difficult adjacent areas, for example, your chest and back are relaxed when you tense your abdomen), you may want to try reverse mode. In this challenging variation, you tense all of your body except one particular target area. For example, tense everything except your chest (while inhaling), hold briefly, then exhale while relaxing everything.

Persistence in this kind of work can lead to inconceivable freedom and mental/physical subtlety. In combative applications, the Russian military operatives who have undergone this training can easily perform tasks which pose seeming contradictory requirements for gentleness vs. strength: disabling an attacker while cradling or protecting a small child; opening a door quietly while drawing and firing a handgun, striking or immobilizing an opponent while maintaining control of a speeding vehicle, and so on.

Here is a list of the more difficult combinations, that includes some combinations for reverse mode work:

Right leg; pause; exhale; relax completely.
Whole body except right leg; pause; exhale; relax completely.
Left leg; pause; exhale; relax completely.
Whole body except left leg; pause; exhale; relax completely.
Right arm; pause; exhale; relax completely.
Whole body except right arm; pause; exhale; relax completely.
Left arm; pause; exhale; relax completely.
Whole body except left arm; pause; exhale; relax completely.
Right arm and right leg only; pause; exhale; relax completely.
Left arm and left leg only; pause; exhale; relax completely.
Left arm and right leg only; pause; exhale; relax completely.
Right arm and left leg only; pause; exhale; relax completely.
Entire right half of body only; pause; exhale; relax completely.
Entire left half of body only; pause; exhale; relax completely.
Right hand (fist) only; pause; exhale; relax completely.
Left hand (fist) only; pause; exhale; relax completely.

Breathing through Body Segments

We now turn to a very special kind of breathing. This advanced work will give you an overview of the physiological basis of Systema Breathing, as explained in Chapter 3. For more details and elaboration on the practices described here, please locate a certified instructor of Systema Breathing.

Imagine you are taking air directly into the cells of the body parts below, and exhaling back through them directly. In contrast to the tension methods described earlier, this work is done with the body entirely relaxed throughout – while exhaling, pausing, and inhaling the breath.

You can perform a minimum of 2 – 3 full cycles (inhale, exhale) for each of the segment pairs below, in the sequence indicated.

1) Inhale through both arms – Exhale through both legs, and vice versa
2) Inhale through left leg – Exhale through right leg and vice versa
3) Inhale through left arm - Exhale through right arm, and vice versa
4) Inhale through left side (arm and leg) - Exhale through right side, and vice versa
5) Inhale through solar plexus - Exhale through arms and legs (simultaneously), and vice versa
6) Inhale through chest - Exhale through back (chest area), and vice versa
7) Inhale through lower abdomen - Exhale through kidneys, and vice versa
8) Inhale through head - Exhale through tailbone, and vice versa
9) Inhale through lower abdomen - Exhale through back of the head, and vice versa
10) Inhale through face - Exhale through kidneys, and vice versa
11) Inhale through liver - Exhale through spleen, and vice versa

12) Inhale through left kidney - Exhale through right kidney, and vice versa
13) Inhale through bladder - Exhale through anus, and vice versa
14) Inhale through both arms - Exhale through both legs, and vice versa

Feeling the Pulse

After a session of "wave" tension and "segmented" tension breathing work you will feel very energized and active. To restore full balance, Systema Breathing has an effective procedure for returning to a quiet body and peaceful mind. This process smoothes and unifies the energy that has been gained through the more vigorous physical work. This leads to the wholeness and harmony of mind, body, and spirit that is the final goal of Systema Breathing. The work presented here is an extension and refinement of one part of the Fundamental Practice of Relaxed Breathing introduced in Chapter 4.

The sensation of "pulse" in the body is the perception of blood as it is pushed through the vessels by the action of the heart. Your pulse can easily be felt with your fingers, or doctor's fingers, at your wrist, at the large arteries of the neck, and at the joining of large vessels in other body areas. In Systema Breathing, we learn to perceive our pulse directly with our minds, in every part of the body. Persistence in this practice builds tremendous sensitivity and awareness of all body functions. It can also lead to deeper awareness of the subtle spiritual phenomena that surround us.

The practice is simple. Lie on your back on the floor, with arms extended relaxed along your sides. Take a minute or so simply to get comfortable, and try to release any obvious tension in your body. Breathe slowly, naturally, and evenly, according to the applicable Principles of Systema Breathing (Chapter 3).

You will probably be able to feel your pulse directly (with your attention only, without moving your fingers or hands to check) in certain areas, such as the heart region and perhaps your neck. But your goal is to learn to feel that same pulsing sensation anywhere in your body.

One way to work with this concept is to begin with your head and slowly work your way down your body. You bring a region into your attention and check whether you can perceive your own pulse in that spot. It can be very subtle at first, so don't get discouraged. You might begin with your scalp, temples, face, or neck (if you intend to work downwards), or even your entire head. Take a minute or so to sense the pulse in that area, continuing to breathe evenly throughout the process. Then you can move to the next lower or adjacent area. At first, the pulse may be more directly perceptible to you in your joints, such as the neck, wrist, groin, and back of the knees. But with practice you will gradually acquire the ability to sense your pulse in any section of your body.

After you have gradually worked downward through your entire body, feeling each separate pulsing region, you can finish the cycle by unifying the many smaller pulses you have already felt in each region into a single larger perception – the pulse of your entire body. It feels as if you are chaining all the separate small pulses together, and your whole body feels unified.

Below is a sample guide for learning to work your way downward through your body. This list is only a guide. The beauty of Systema Breathing is that every practitioner will walk his own path to harmony and mastery. You are the best judge of your own limitations. You may wish to adopt the list below as a general guide, and then adapt the program in certain areas, where you may wish to work in greater detail, with a more refined perception of subparts in a given region. Or you may choose to combine the pulse feeling of several adjacent subparts into one unified sensation. After any such modification, you can resume the suggested program for the rest of your practice session.

Suggested Pulse Perception Sequence [Example program]

1) Temples
2) Neck
3) Heart
4) Navel
5) Groin
6) Knees
7) Ankles
8) Toes
9) Unite all the areas

At first, you will probably notice that your pulse can be more easily felt in your heart than in the other areas. Over time, you will become more sensitive to that same sensation anywhere in the body. The final stage of "Unite all the areas" means that ultimately you feel a single pulse beat that resonates through every organ, every limb, reaching every cell of your body. To attain that, when you have completed all the subparts, spend a few minutes trying to unify or chain all the local sub-pulses into a single pulse feeling.

End the practice by taking several additional even and complete breaths, then gradually begin to move yourself gently, and sit up with breathing. The pulse work described here fosters incredible sensitivity and awareness, both internal and external, that can be applied to improving your health and to better accomplishing any kind of work.

Chapter Nine

Conclusion

"Whoever has seen any place, or has described it and has said in his heart, "There, that is the place, and that is all," has really sinned against the Spirit" - Stephen Graham ("Undiscovered Russia", 1912)

We've covered a lot of ground. I wonder how many breaths you've taken since you began reading this book?

The material taught here would suffice for a lifetime of challenging and rewarding work. It's tempting to think that this is all. Even this section's name, "Conclusion", hints that we have wrapped up a complete package here. But we haven't. Systema Breathing work is endlessly profound. There are additional practices and there is much more to be harvested from the work that we've already covered. But we have to end somewhere. So I'll offer a few further thoughts on the benefits you can expect from your new practice of Systema Breathing, and then we'll finish with a "final exam".

This work can help you in many ways. The most important harvest is improvement in your everyday life. For example, from the "breath holding" practice, you can learn to raise the threshold for instinctive panic in stressful situations. This is because regular practice of the Russian Breathing Method increases your physical and psychological reserves, develops your self-control, and develops your understanding of yourself and those around you. Someone who regularly practices this system gradually develops a kind of positive shield against fear, stress, pain, and fatigue. This allows your body to stay comfortable all the time.

Sometime after you begin this work, you'll find yourself attempting to lift an object whose weight you have misjudged, something that is actually far heavier than you had realized. Without the training, without correct breathing, your stiff body might have struggled uselessly with the weight, resulting in a strained or injured back. But having practiced these methods for a while, you'll surprise yourself by instead maintaining an even and sufficient breath as your muscles smoothly adapt to the unexpected condition. In the end, you'll find yourself easily hoisting what might have been impossible for you before.

If you are a student or professional worker engaged in a lot of thinking for long periods, your breath can help to re-distribute your stagnant or unbalanced energies. By doing some exercises or just the simple 'wave' breathing taught in Chapter 8 of this book, you can naturally and quickly re-harmonize your physical and mental energies throughout your body. When you sustain any injury or feel any pain in a particular organ or limb, breathe into and through the affected area to quickly relieve pain and speed healing. With a certain period of practice you'll find that your digestion has improved.

When driving, you'll find yourself calmer, more focused, and less distracted by random thoughts of all your issues and problems that you can't solve at that moment. You'll find yourself becoming a safer driver, with better awareness and you'll be less likely to get upset at other drivers or traffic conditions. With time you'll begin to sense how to regulate your own breath to handle any special need. Just as one example (you'll discover many others on your own!), if you begin to feel fatigued while driving, you can use very rapid breathing to keep yourself fully alert as you drive to the next safe rest stop.

Your body weight will reset to its natural optimum point, as your mind naturally calms down and nervous eating is reduced. This calming effect will extend to your sleep and once again, a balance of just the right amount of sleep, without deficiency or excess, will be achieved. Excess tension can spark a vicious cycle of sleeplessness and fatigue leading to accumulation of additional tension. Sometimes insomnia is due to uncontrolled or unconscious tension, which is greatly reduced through the practice of Systema Breathing.

The reduction of tension throughout the body will have benefits for your face as well. Excess tension registers on the face and causes the appearance of premature aging. With proper breathing, your tension will begin to dissolve and along with it, any lines of stress, fatigue and displeasure that we imprint on our own appearance. In fact, your skin will greatly benefit from this practice. The skin is an extension of our Nervous System. Because proper breathing regulates and harmonizes our thoughts, calms us, and provides better oxygenation, the Nervous System's natural healing reaction extends to the skin as well. Thus, your skin will naturally begin to have a healthy color and to appear smoother and younger.

But beyond all these immediate improvements in your life, the greatest benefits may come to your psyche and spirit. Centuries ago, William Blake wrote the inspirational poem "Pentecost":

> Unless the eye catch fire, then God will not be seen,
> Unless the ear catch fire, then God will not be heard,
> Unless the tongue catch fire, then God will not be named,
> Unless the heart catch fire, then God will not be loved,
> Unless the mind catch fire, then God will not be known.

Now that you've read the poem, as your "final exam" for this book please answer the question below for yourself:

What does a fire need?

Interviews

Interview with Kwan Lee

Kwan is a Senior Systema Instructor for Vladimir Vasiliev and Mikhail Ryabko and is the Director of Russian Martial Art Arizona. He is also the Chief Mechanical Engineer for ExecuSpec Inc. and a Senior Analyst for the U.S. Army's Future Combat Systems Program.

Q: What have you learned about the roots and history of the Russian Orthodox Church and its traditional practices that might help lay people, non-Russians and non-specialists to get a glimmer of understanding of this profound culture and faith?

A: It has been said that the healthy soul is constantly returning to a state of wonder and awe. Without humility, we cannot be truly awed, and when we are incapable of becoming awed, we fail to be inspired. When we lack inspiration, we generally lack hope. Humility plays an essential role in Systema Breathing. To understand the heart of this method, one must look to the heart of the Christian Orthodox Faith.

Orthodox Russians have adhered to a very practical way of belief that has been thriving since the First Century; an existential fusion of theology and the Unknown that facilitates the participation in the mysteries of God while emphasizing a humble and clean Earthly and church-going existence denoted by scripture and Holy Tradition.

While many in the non-Orthodox world would attribute the worst sins as being corporal, the one thing to understand about Orthodoxy is its condemnation of pride as the life-killing and most egregious sin. Also high on the list is the lack of hope, or despair. To combat such formidable adversaries, the Faith provides a comprehensive way of life centered on humility.

The church is a pivotal part of an Orthodox Christian's life, and even its architecture is designed to command respect for things Holy. When walking into a traditionally built Russian Orthodox church, we can immediately feel that the floor plan and services performed take the focus off of ourselves and help us to be mindful of why we are there. Everywhere around us, we see Holy icons, strategically placed to expedite the connection between the faithful and God. Each is free to walk around the building during services to make offerings of lit candles and make prayers, venerating the saints and Holy figures depicted through icons. The beautifully constructed and ornamented churches and chapels remind the faithful of the immense beauty in the Kingdom of Heaven and serve to put those that enter the grounds into a state of awe and humility.

There are no benches in a Russian Orthodox Church (except for a couple for the elderly and the sick). The entire two or more hours of service are done standing up, so that the participants are more attuned to the spiritual work of the prayers.

Prayer is a very important aspect of Orthodox life. In and out of the church, throughout the day, beautiful prayers, which usually begin and end with a humble supplication to God, are recited that articulate everything from remembrance to poignant pleas for mercy. For many in Russia who lived through the atrocities of war and the evils of the Soviet regime, praying to God became the only solace in life. Their conviction doubled as they silently and secretly prayed with humility in a world bereft of hope.

This prayer life continues today in homes, churches, chapels, and monasteries as Orthodoxy again takes its place at the forefront of Russian life.

Centuries ago, a group of ascetic Orthodox monks perfected a way of prayer that utilized specific breathing methods in a practice called Hesychasm, and to this day, their system of breathing and posture is used in prayer to facilitate a deeper connection with God. Systema Breathing is based on many of these breathing practices.

Q: In what ways has your practice of Systema Breathing reinforced your spirituality or informed your Christian understanding?

A: It should be obvious by now that Systema and Breathing Method as taught by Vladimir and Mikhail are deeply faith-based and require a good bit of humility in order to achieve any degree of success. As with the Hesychastic methods of breathing, I have found that Mikhail's breathing methods have helped serve a similar purpose in my prayer life.

In performing these exercises over the first year, my body began to know more of its potential, and I was able to develop greater awareness and control over it. With practice, not only was I able to function better in the combative aspects of Systema, but I was also able to use this awareness and control in prayer to get into a zone of complete concentration, with my mind less distracted and the residual tensions within my body gradually melted away. Prayer became a more heightened and illuminated mental state–a concerted and harmonized effort, which serves to unlock the doors to the heart.

There is a peaceful centering to this Breathing Method that begins to affect all areas of your life. The process is like polishing a lens to remove all aberrations so that there is complete clarity and focus on what you are choosing to look at.

Q: Conversely, what insights from spirituality can you offer that might help people understand the breath training?

A: St. Makariy of Optina Monastery advises in the following way:

"Pray simply. Do not expect to find in your heart any remarkable gift of prayer. Consider yourself unworthy of it. Then you will find peace."

You could almost change out "prayer" with "breathing" or "pray" with "breathe." Perhaps this is the humility that drives us to ask God's help in those times when we can no longer hold or maintain our breath (in this work and in the other areas of our lives).

We often choose to rely solely on our own strength and wit to pull us through hard times or to break through the limits of our abilities. Usually, what we can muster on our own falls drastically short of what is truly attainable. This is especially true with Systema Breathing. As Vladimir and Mikhail teach, the best way to go past these uncomfortable ceilings is to trust in God and humbly ask for help when we meet the toughest parts of the exercises (or life). I have found that if you push yourself to a point of utter powerlessness, you will have the opportunity to expand your potential by just asking God for mercy. It actually has a calming effect. You will become more relaxed and less fearful of proceeding further. The process is simple but very enlightening, and I am constantly amazed at the results I see in myself and in others when we give ourselves completely over to it.

Q: As a teacher of "Systema", the Russian martial art training what have you found to be the most difficult or challenging aspect of Systema Breathing for new students to learn, and what have you found most effective in helping new students overcome those initial hurdles?

A: We all have days when the work is enjoyable and other days when the work is unusually tough to grasp or perform due to a mental block, lack of sleep, poor conditioning of unused muscle groups, or just plain laziness or fatigue. If you have an inquisitive mind, a humble attitude, and a bit of dedication, you will do very well.

Outside of its use in daily life, I can see the culmination of Systema Breathing in its application to training. When you take a few blows to the solar plexus, you find very quickly that the principles of this Method can help you overcome your fears of getting hit as well as dispersing the shock and related pain. It is fascinating how adaptable Systema really is to virtually any human situation or task ranging from resting to fighting.

As for the difficulties in Systema Breathing that I have noticed in new students, I would say that a big hurdle is a problem with perception.

Most novice students find it hard to see the breathing process as something material enough to control and the breath as something that can be "pushed through" tense spots of the body. Here, specific action is as important as visualization. As Mikhail suggests for the beginner, making the breath audible or slightly restricting it will give the breath substance and a transportable quality. You will see this as you experiment with these ideas in a variety of physical scenarios.

Many students choose to leave the work in the gym and forget that these breathing methods should be applied throughout the day for maximum results. There is conditioning that builds with continued application of these exercises, and it is important that you find ways to fit them into your schedule.

Finally, I have noticed, especially in the West, that we have been conditioned by society to marginalize the role of God in our lives to such an extent that many tend to close up when they are asked to pray to God in training. If this is a problem for you, and you would still like a glimpse of the effects of how pleading for mercy can impact this training, try it just a few times - take yourself to the breaking point in one of the breath-holding exercises and start saying 'Lord have mercy" in your mind. Do not let pride prevent you from doing this, you will be glad you tried.

Q: You have trained in Russia on several occasions. What people or events particularly struck you there and deepened your understanding of the work?

A: Without singling out a specific event, I would say that the people that we met within Mikhail's circle (and many outside of it) were remarkably genuine and warm. The main difference that I noticed is that, more often than in my experiences in the States, once training began, the people did not change. If the person were naturally serious in demeanor, he/she had this attitude in training, and if the person had a great sense of humor, this manifested itself as well. There was no need to invite excess tension into our bodies by trying to be something else–no need to imitate a monkey, mantis, or marsupial, in order to be effective. To me, this reinforced the idea in Russian Martial Art that we must train as human beings and be honest in our work in every way–to live and train without delusion, with love for one another, and with true reverence to the Holy.

Russians, especially Mikhail's students, are a very faithful, loyal, and persevering people – an inspiring model for living Systema in and out of the training hall.

Q: What advice would you give to a person approaching the practice of Systema Breathing for the first time?

A: The path is simple, but the work can be tough psychologically, at times pushing you into very challenging territory. Never give up. Sometimes it is necessary to endure a bit of chaos to get to the underlying truths represented in Systema Breathing. If you keep an open mind and experiment outside of the basic guidelines, you will enjoy the work even more.

Also, as with prayer, there is a discipline involved in securing the necessary time to devote to this work. Make an effort to find that time throughout your day and immerse yourself completely. Be diligent with the exercises, but increase the intensity gradually lest you may push yourself too hard and burn out before realizing your potential.

Finally, do not be lazy. As the masters say, try not to like yourself too much and you will succeed!

"Breathing is the foundation of life" An interview with Vladimir Vasiliev

- Russian Special Operations Unit professional
- Director and chief instructor of Russian Martial Art outside of Russia
- Has personally trained and certified over 100 Systema instructors worldwide
- Currently running Systema Headquarters school in Toronto, Canada

Q: Do you teach breathing to all your martial arts students, from the onset of their training, or is it considered to be more advanced work for later, when students have developed a foundation in other skills?

A: Not only do I begin with breathing, from the very first lesson, but I'm actually obligated to present breathing right away, to all people who train with me. If a student is not prepared with proper breathing, then no matter what other skills he has, he's going to get burned. If you lack proper breathing, no techniques will ever rescue you. Breath is also essential for endurance, depending on the amount of time involved. While a typical fight might last a few seconds or a few minutes, combat in a battle can go on for a long, long time. And breathing applies to everyone – not only professional soldiers or athletes. We are all challenged with stresses from all sides, every moment we're alive. Every stress, whether psychological or physical, inhibits or interferes with breathing in some way. So we have to know how to deal with that – we have to know how to control interruptions of breathing as they happen. Once the stress is gone, we then have to know how to recuperate. Proper breathing is the ideal way to recuperate, because our breath is always right there with us. And if you breathe properly, even before the stress begins, you create a huge energy reserve in your body. Then it becomes a lot harder to throw you off.

Q: What is the most important personal quality for a person to achieve mastery of breathing?

A: It's the same quality that underlies most other skills – humility. That's what we all need. Humility allows us to understand ourselves. It opens us up to God, and to everything positive that the world can give us. Then the skill just flows in. Humility with hard work allows you to achieve everything.

One of the Church Fathers has said it so well: you may have so many virtues and skills that if you write a zero for every one of them, you could fill up a whole book. Imagine a whole book filled with zeros! And unless you have a 'one' or any other number in front of the zeros – that is all that they will ever be – nothing. That 'number' is humility, it gives true value to all our virtues, skills and achievements.

Q: While training in the more demanding and strenuous aspects of Systema Breathing, I've sometimes heard the advice "Don't like yourself too much". This is interesting for North Americans, because our modern culture emphasizes self-love and self-esteem above everything. Can you explain this part of the teaching a bit further?

A: Liking ourselves is good, because we are all creatures of God, and we should like all Creation, including ourselves. That is fundamental. But if you like yourself more than necessary, you kill yourself. It's like medicine – just a couple extra drops of an otherwise good medication can kill you. The same applies to self-pity and self-liking. There is a fine balance. If you like yourself to the point that you consider yourself better or more important than others, then that becomes injurious – you've stepped over a boundary. Beware of pride, vanity and egotism. Consider others to be better than you and be glad for them that they are. With God's help it will make your training and your life very productive and happy.

Q: At what age can a child or anyone begin to train in Systema Breathing?

A: There is no minimum age. As soon as the baby is born, you can teach the baby. The baby observes you and naturally imitates everything you do. For example, as we breathe properly while caring for our baby, she's watching us and she instinctively begins to breathe the same way. So it starts immediately. As the child grows, you can start explaining things to him or her. You can also make your breathing audible, so that he or she can understand more. Kids are usually very receptive to that, they really enjoy it. Hopefully this would be taught well before the age when a child becomes a bit rebellious or confrontational with the parents. Then they won't feel they're doing the breathing because you told them to, but rather they will have seen the value of it all along, by themselves. This will strengthen the parent-child relationship.

Q: I have an active young friend who smokes, but claims that his smoking does not affect his breath or his athletic endurance. In your view, is this possible?

A: This reminds me of myself, when I was 18 and also a smoker. At that time I was undergoing specialized military training, and one of the tasks was to chase down my 'opponent' as we tracked many kilometers across huge open snow fields on cross-country skis. I was required to carry a full military supply pack, with a complete load of ammunition and other heavy equipment. Though I didn't know it at the time, my 'opponent' was a ski Master, a real professional athlete. My assignment was not to lose track of him and to follow as closely as possible. Like your friend, I was completely confident that I was in top physical shape, though I smoked at that time. But since I'd never had any physical difficulties with any task, my confidence in my own condition was absolute. The distance was moderate, only 5 kilometers, but that ski Master worked like a ski machine! It was unbelievably difficult for me to keep up with him. I was shocked to find that for a few minutes in the final stages, I was barely able to function.

When we came to a stop, I sat in the snow completely drained and (as I was told later) my face went through all possible colors of exhaustion from red to white to blue and yellow.

I thought to myself – what if this had been a real battle, and I had no time to recover? I felt I'd be useless in that situation. As I sprawled out at the finish line, utterly depleted, I pulled the cigarette pack from my pocket and buried it in the snow. I never touched cigarettes again.

Q: If somebody is sick or injured, should they attempt to practice Systema Breathing or should they wait until they are completely recovered?

A: You should start breath training as soon as you hear about it, no matter whether you are healthy or sick. Breathing is one of your strongest tools to bring yourself to recovery. There are so many restrictions and limitations in our bodies, even before we get sick or injured. Even in healthy people, the connections between different muscles groups can become disrupted. That's why even healthy people often don't move smoothly – their movements come out jerky. Breathing breaks through the restrictions and barriers and allows the muscle groups to connect evenly. What's most important is that proper breathing prevents disruption and destruction in the body. Breathing constructs internal alignments in the body so that injury becomes almost impossible. This applies to the external framework, the muscular-skeletal system, as well as the internal organs and immune system.

There are many kinds of movement. Sometimes even when we are externally constrained due to injury, breath finds a way to move through the body from the inside. The same applies to internal problems and sickness. The breath creates internal pathways for directing the body's natural healing energy. This may not be a conventional scientific explanation but in practice it works. You need to try it, work with it, and feel it. We could spend a lot of time describing and explaining some kind of good fruit, but if you never taste it, you won't get the benefits of having it.

Q: Can you explain in a bit more detail or give an example of how that healing process works in practice?

A: Yes, there are a huge number of examples from my own teaching. At one of my recent martial arts training seminars, there was a student who was an experienced martial artist but who'd never really learned any correct concepts of breathing before. This seminar was his first exposure to Systema Breathing. But he grabbed the idea, applied it, and was successful. This is how it happened.

This man had experienced hip injuries in the past. At the very start of the seminar, somehow he fell onto his hip, and re-injured himself to the point that he wasn't able to walk. Since he was determined to watch the rest of the training, he had to be wheeled back into the seminar room in an office chair. It looked a bit funny, but he was in serious pain. He was unable to train, so I told him to begin breathing through the injured area. Inhale through the injury, exhale back out through it. At first, he had doubts about it. He took a few breaths, but then he just sat there, watching. So I went up to him again and told him "If you trust me, you've got to do this for real, really work at it! Breathe in and out through the injured area – work hard at it." So this time, he began working seriously with his pain. He concentrated intently on this, and he kept breathing that way for about two hours. Not doing anything else, just breathing through that injured area. After two hours, he stood up and started walking, as if nothing had happened! He felt warmth flowing through his whole body. This was the warmth of the healing energy that we all have. He was shocked and amazed. I'm sure he'll continue this for the rest of his life.

Q: If we learn primarily from a book, a video, or a single seminar, and if we lack constant supervision and correction from an actual Master of Systema Breathing, can we still benefit from our practice, even though we may not be performing the Method perfectly all the time?

A: Yes, absolutely. You will always benefit from your practice. By nature, all people are self-educating. We always instruct ourselves – this is natural and perfect. You will also develop new insights and concepts that are beneficial for yourself and others. If you pray and join your own forces to God's power, you'll be on the right track from the beginning.

Q: Why do we need special methods and practices beyond prayer and church attendance? If all the power is in prayer and in God, why can't we just go to Church or just pray simply, as directed in the Gospel of Matthew?

A: We must understand that we have been given both the soul and the body. With all the spiritual practices, we are certainly not denying the importance of the body. Health and physical strength are needed for our life, for the very gathering of the Holy Spirit. The spirit has to prevail but God gave us the body as well. Even in our prayers we ask for health of both the soul and the body.

On the other hand, we don't know how to pray properly and we don't go to church in the right way. Prayer has to be combined with humility, fighting with our own weaknesses and good deeds throughout our lives, otherwise it has little benefit. It becomes just words. Going to church isn't merely a mystic ritual. A mystic ritual is something that doesn't depend on what you do during the rest of your life. In a ritual you can just walk in, go through certain mechanical procedures, say certain word sequences, and these alone are supposed to help you. But prayer is not like that. Your soul has to be ready, your heart should be clear and then prayer functions as it should – it connects you to God. To do this, we can use physical aids to help us, and breathing is one of them, as well as training, and all our other good activities. Any good deed you do turns you towards God, and any bad deed that you do turns you away from Him. Any time you work hard, and try to overcome your weaknesses, is a major progress for personal growth and it brings you closer to God. Breathing is a perfect example of an arena where you can work hard, and where you can fight your self-pity, weakness and pride. If you work in that way, every breath you take will serve the purpose of praising the Lord.

The Russian word for 'air' is 'vozdooh'. It literally means 'a heap of spirit'. This helps us understand that if you learn to inhale not only air, but to gather the Spirit, that's when you are really alive.

Interview with Mikhail Ryabko – The Master Teacher of the Systema Combative and Health method.

- Founder and chief instructor of Systema
- 25 years of service with Special Operations Unit
- Tactical commander of hostage rescue teams, counter-terrorist operations and armed criminal neutralization
- A Colonel, holding many government medals and awards
- Advisor to the Minister of Justice of Russia

Q: Why do you so heavily emphasize breath training?

A: Breathing is the most fundamental function of our body. It plays the key role in most of our physiological and psychological processes. If we learn to control our breathing, we essentially learn to control all functions of our body and psyche.

Q: What physical and spiritual changes will occur to the student as he begins to practice Systema Breathing?

A: The first change will be better health. Correct breathing done with our Systema exercises immediately strengthens the body and begins to eliminate pathogens and physical imbalances of all kinds. All of our students notice this very soon after they begin training. At the same time, a deeper process of cleansing begins. Psychological and spiritual impurities are removed by this practice. As impurities are shed, there is more room for God's pure spirit to dwell within the student. The student's mind, heart, and soul will naturally begin to turn more towards God.

Q: Many people are curious about Systema Breathing practice of holding your breath. Can you tell us more on the rationale underlying these particular practices? What is the

difference between holding the breath when performed as an exercise as opposed to when it is done under stress, under duress, or unconsciously?

A: In many areas of life we can see a difference between doing something correctly with a willing heart compared to being forced or imposed on in any way. For a very basic example, sex is very positive physically and psychologically for a loving couple, and totally damaging if imposed by force in case of rape. We undertake the breathing practice, using our free will, as given by God, thus the effects are only positive.
Here is what happens. When we experience something that we perceive to be stressful and hold our breath, on a physiological level our blood vessels constrict, circulation is impaired and our cells are deprived of nourishment – oxygen and food. When this stress reaction takes place at a high intensity or when it happens consistently it leads to gradual destruction of the body, to aging, injuries and disease.

When we hold our breath as part of the breath training, we do it willingly, so there is no psychological stress. Thus, there is no blood vessel constriction, and quite the opposite, the blood vessels dilate in a normal response to a healthy exercise. Therefore, the effect of such training is beneficial in every way physically and psychologically.

Q: What kinds of lifestyle and daily life habits are best to go along with Systema Breathing and are most conducive to our development and progress in all aspects of life?

A: The student needs to be a normal, good, and decent person. Students should not be looking for miracles, but carry on their daily life in a kind and upright fashion. It is necessary to fulfill all proper duties (and miracles will occur when they are needed). Students may someday have to fight for their country, and they should always be true to their families, stay away from drugs, from smoking and generally clean up and harmonize their lives with the principles and directions that God has provided to human beings.

In times of extreme stress, people will naturally pray. In cases of terrible illness, severe accidents, terrorist attack, or when nursing a sick child, everybody, regardless of their superficial spiritual beliefs, will turn to God in prayer. But why only at those extreme moments? The problem is that we don't want to owe anything to God. When everything is going well, we attribute all achievements to ourselves. Some people even think they have special powers – that they can freely control themselves and the whole universe. But even if something as simple as diarrhea hits, the person immediately grabs the pills. If the pills don't help, and the problem is very serious, everyone naturally turns to, or at least acknowledges God. Our practice should broaden that and turn us more fully to God under all conditions.

We have been teaching the correct breathing program. How deep the student goes with it is up to his free will. Everyone needs to choose whether to join with the high or the low powers.

Q: Can you discuss the link between breathing and spirituality in more detail?

A: Prayer brings us to God. Getting closer to God is like coming up to a river of love and light of such intensity that if the body and psyche are not properly prepared, it can rip you apart! The body is strengthened, purified, and prepared for prayer by proper breathing practice. The body has a natural state of strength, health, and purity, when it is ready for God's presence. The ideal blood pressure is 120/80. The ideal body temperature taken underarm is 36 degrees Celsius (96.8 degrees Fahrenheit). The ideal pulse rate is 60 beats per minute. Under stress, all these measures will rise. When these parameters are lowered, we are able to perceive God. God comes to us naturally when we feel calm, when we're asleep, or when we see the spirit realms in a coma. Breathing and prayer both help to lower these crucial physiological measures. Whereas, stress, anger, fear, resentment, etc. make our blood pressure, heart rate and temperature rise. This makes us open to the evil forces or energies, and brings destruction. In general, the correct practice of breathing strengthens and purifies the body and spirit. When combined with prayer, this eventually brings true happiness because we become one with God.

May God bless you!

Mikhail Ryabko with his Special Operations group en-route to a mission.

LET EVERY BREATH...
is published with the blessing of
Reverend Father Vladimir Malchenko,
of Holy Trinity Russian Orthodox Church
Toronto, Canada

Notes

Notes

Notes